SATAN'S
Lullaby

SATAN'S
Lullaby

*An Eye-Opening Look at Satan's Subtle Schemes
and God's Plan for Overcoming Them*

By Jon Harrell

Unless otherwise noted, all Scripture quotations are taken from the King James Version (KJV) of the Holy Bible.

HGR
Editorial Services

Edited by the HGR Editorial Services

Homer G. Rhea, Editor
Nellie Keasling, Copy Editor
Lonna Gattenby, Layout and Cover Design
homer8238@gmail.com

ISBN: 978-1-59684-968-6

Published by Derek Press
Cleveland, TN 37311
Printed in the United States of America

DEDICATION

To my parents, for the continual love and support that has always kept me and my family, and for the foundation of Christianity they have taught me my entire life.

To my mother-in-law who received me as one of her own and has instilled the very same values as did my parents.

To my late father-in-law who was a true example of a follower of Christ and finished well.

TABLE OF CONTENTS

FOREWORD

As Christians, I think all of us have, at some point, or even at the present, struggled with our faith. As a young teen who had recently received Christ as my Savior, I struggled with the reality of God. The Enemy pointed out that I had no tangible evidence to prove the existence of God. The struggle was real for me until, through the study of the Word, and growing in my relationship with Christ, I began to understand where it was all coming from. It was always interesting to me that Satan would try to convince me God was not real, but my Enemy never tried to convince me he did not exist. I began to realize this was a scheme of Satan to destroy my faith in God so that he ultimately and eternally could separate me from God.

In this book, Jon Harrell begins to open to us the warfare we are in. When we are saved, we step into a realm of spiritual warfare. Therefore, we need to understand where the war is coming from and the tactics that are used against us. This book does just that as the author uses the Word of God and personal stories to enlighten us about the snares of our Enemy. Jon is a living testimony to all he has written here. I have personally witnessed his journey of growth from a young, single man to his life now.

This book is a tremendous study for new converts, as well as those of us who have served the Lord for many years. We are always growing and learning so that we may come into full maturity in Christ! The purpose of God for our lives is to conform us to the image of Christ. He enables us to live victoriously in this life so that we can live eternally in the life to come.

Thomas L. Powell
Administrative Bishop
Missouri Church of God
State Executive Offices

ACKNOWLEDGMENTS

I wish to acknowledge a few people whose help was critical to the writing of this book.

- First, my wife, Jennifer: Thank you so much for your continued love and support and the tremendous sacrifice of time that you committed to this project.

- Second, my family: Jennifer, Jordan, Jesse, Josh, and Jentzen: Thank you for being my audience the many times we worked together through the corrections and changes of this book. I suppose you may have it memorized by now. I love you guys with all my heart.

- Third, the many people who read the rough draft as a favor: Thank you all for your time and for your suggestions which were influential in developing this book.

SATAN'S *Lullaby*

12

INTRODUCTION

At first, I thought of this book as a divine accident; I couldn't explain it any other way. Since then, many things have happened that have caused me to change my viewpoint. Several lives have been transformed because of this book, including mine. Now, I call it a gift.

I started to work on *Satan's Lullaby* in 2001, when I moved to central Georgia and accepted the pastorate of a small church. My first mission was to present my view on the basics of Christianity, which I did through a sermon series. My goal was for this series to serve as a refresher course for the seasoned Christians, and also as an introduction to Christianity for the new converts. As I began to study for the sermon series, I was overwhelmed by the amount of material I collected. Finally, I concluded that I must not only preach through this sermon series, but if I were to sufficiently cover this topic, I also needed to compile this material in a book. I had never entertained the thought of becoming a writer. It seemed there were already countless books available on this subject. Yet, I still felt the urge to write about the topic from my perspective. I believed that God's message needed to be presented in a way that was relevant and easy to understand.

My first inclination was to write a book for my own use and for those to whom I personally ministered. With little inspiration at first, I questioned the value of such a work. I was indecisive about how to approach the book. However, one day, while enjoying a day off, I turned on the computer and just started putting my notes into a format that might make sense to a reader. I was uncertain I would ever complete this work, but just wanted to take a stab at it. Soon, I began to feel many of the frustrations that I'm sure most authors deal with. The thought entered my mind: *This isn't worth the trouble!* As I contemplated deleting the file I had just created, the doorbell rang. Standing at the door were two well-dressed women. They began to share a false doctrine in an attempt to pull me into their religion. I found myself making numerous statements that came directly from this nine-week sermon series that I had just wrapped up. What I didn't expect was the tremendous immediate impact that it would have on one of the women. It was so powerful that the other woman physically moved between me and the woman and pushed her away backwards from my porch. I was left standing there in disbelief. That moment revealed to me the value of the work I had been doing.

For the first time, lack of inspiration began to fade. It was truly a foundational moment. Having had a real conversation that helped me know where to start, I began typing away at a first draft. Over the next year, I spent countless hours reading and rereading, writing and rewriting. The book really began taking shape. During this process, however, I allowed obsession to take the place of my initial inspiration. I began to take ownership of this book, which in reality, belonged to God. I realized I needed to step away from the project to regain some perspective, or even to just let it go. I quit working on it, placed it in a folder, and put it completely out of my mind.

Several years went by, some good, but others very difficult. Ministry was taking a toll on me, but it was also inspiring me. I eventually followed my dream of planting a church. To generate income during this process, I decided to delve into the housing market. It would be an understatement to say that I had my hands full. The timing, however, was horrible. I began building with no idea of what was just around the corner. Having invested in the housing market just prior to the market crash, my family and I lost everything.

We spent the next five years gathering the broken pieces and starting over. Getting back on my feet was extremely hard. I don't think that most people who knew me understood how financially destroyed I was. This was hard for a person who probably once had too much self-confidence. What I didn't know, was how much this difficulty would shape me into a better person. I had forgotten that I had written about this kind of change long before I had experienced it myself.

I finally recovered enough to afford a sufficient home once again for my family of six. Soon after that, a door of ministry opportunity opened at a church where I had previously served. It was while moving boxes out of storage to take back to my old office that I ran across a copy of the book. I had not laid eyes on it in years. In fact, the first draft was now more than twelve years old. I had forgotten most of its content. Just to reminisce, I began looking through it. As I read page after page, the content pierced my heart. I felt as if God had me to write this book for me, even before I knew I needed it. I made an altar out of the bumper of my vehicle and found myself fighting back tears. I realized that my experiences had led me through the process about which I had already written. It wasn't just my own words; God was speaking to me. At that point, it became clear to me just how important it was to complete the book and get it into circulation. I knew that others could benefit from it as well. With newfound inspiration and the help of God, I put the final touches on *Satan's Lullaby*.

SATAN'S *Lullaby*

The name of the book came from the title of the original sermon series. To teach on the basics of Christianity, I chose to begin by introducing the villain of the Christian faith. I realize this is not a popular idea for reaching people in a practical way; nonetheless, revealing the origin of the struggle for a believer is imperative to teaching someone how to be an overcomer. Ezekiel 28:12-15 was chosen to be the opening passage, because it is the most comprehensive passage describing Satan prior to his fall. This dual prophecy is found nestled in the verbal description of the king of Tyre who reigned during Ezekiel's day. Many believe that this earthly king was used in the revealing of Satan because of the striking similarity of both personalities. Regardless of why this scripture is written the way it is, it gives us a good foundation for understanding the origin of Satan, which is very important for the discussion that takes place in this book.

If you've ever wanted "CliffsNotes" on the basics of Christianity, this book will be very useful. It moves very fast, so prepare yourself! I hope this book will be an important weapon in your arsenal to gain and maintain victory until the day you will never again have to face an attack of Satan.

—Jon Harrell

PART ONE

Practical Warfare

CHAPTER 1

THE SONG

Son of man, take up a lamentation upon the king of Tyrus, and say unto him, Thus saith the Lord God; Thou sealest up the sum, full of wisdom, and perfect in beauty. Thou hast been in Eden the garden of God; every precious stone was thy covering, the sardius, topaz, and the diamond, the beryl, the onyx, and the jasper, the sapphire, the emerald, and the carbuncle, and gold: the workmanship of thy tabrets and of thy pipes was prepared in thee in the day that thou wast created. Thou art the anointed cherub that covereth; and I have set thee so: thou wast upon the holy mountain of God; thou hast walked up and down in the midst of the stones of fire. Thou wast perfect in thy ways from the day that thou wast created, till iniquity was found in thee (Ezekiel 28:12-15).

Since the beginning of time, no one else has ever been endowed with as much God-given excellence as the person described in this text. This individual seems to exemplify God's perfect creativity. The passage begins with the words, "Thou sealest up the sum, full of wisdom, and perfect in beauty." This is an expression of utter perfection.

It indicates that the person being described has been created to measure up to the highest of God's standards. The words, "Thou sealest up the sum," simply mean that all expected measures of excellence have been met. It should be noted that this is the only person in all of Scripture besides God himself who has been given such a lofty verbal description. This passage does, however, specify that the one being described was created. Therefore, he is neither preexistent nor self-existent. Nonetheless, it is evident God invested an incredible amount of glory and authority into this person. Who could possibly stand so tall, and why would God create such a being? This book will delve into these questions. It will also shed light on how this applies to us, but before we dig in, let's take a quick look at God's purpose for creation in general.

God's Purpose in Creation

> For by him were all things created, that are in heaven, and that are in earth, visible and invisible, whether they be thrones, or dominions, or principalities, or powers: all things were created by him, and for him (Colossians 1:16).

> Thou hast created all things, and for thy pleasure they are and were created (Revelation 4:11).

Both passages tell us the principle reason for creation. We were created for God's purposes—to bring Him glory, honor, and pleasure in all that we do. We were not created for self-indulgence. Nowhere in Scripture do we see God instructing us to analyze our lives to determine what we want for ourselves, or encouragement to follow our own desires. Instead, Scripture gives us instruction to seek out God's will for our lives, as well as specific instruction on how to follow His will.

Throughout the Bible, we are given another purpose for our existence. God desires to have fellowship and enjoyment with us. An example of this occurred when God walked with Adam and Eve in the Garden of Eden. We experience this in the nearness of His presence afforded us by the cross. God reached across a great expanse to mankind to share His love with us. We are His creation. The psalmist said, "Know ye that the LORD he is God: it is he that hath made us, and not we ourselves; we are his people, and the sheep of his pasture (Psalm 100:3)."

This verse indicates that God's purpose also benefits us. He is our Shepherd. Through this, we can understand not only our purpose but also our relationship to God. The person being described in Ezekiel 28 can't escape the fact that he also was created to please God and bring Him glory. He was created with fellowship in mind. However, this individual stands far above the ordinary expression of creativity. Being perfect in beauty and full of wisdom, he is the only individual mentioned in Scripture to whom God attributes the words, "Thou sealest up the sum."

The Creation, Purpose, and Fall of Satan

Ever since sin entered into the world, mankind has been flawed both spiritually and physically. Even before a child is born, the manifestation of death may already begin to appear. Being flawed by sin, the very thing that was intended to be perfect appears imperfect. In contrast, the creature spoken of by Ezekiel was created perfect, but was afterward corrupted. Except for the angels, only Adam and Eve were created perfect, but even they do not fit the description of this creature. An angel is being described, but not just any angel, rather an angel who is called "The anointed cherub that covereth" (v. 14). Let's note that this is a singular position, *the anointed cherub*, meaning that this was the only angel who held this title. In scripture, angels were often pictured covering different items with their wings. Sometimes they covered their feet and face in an act of holiness. They were also pictured covering the mercy seat on the Ark of the Covenant. This "covering" is thought by some to be the guarding of God's attributes such as His holiness or power. Either way, Ezekiel's writing seems to infer that "the anointed cherub that covereth" stood at the highest pinnacle of God's purpose.

This thought is reinforced by the fact that he had been given positional privilege. He had been in the Garden of Eden and on the Holy Mountain of God—the place from where God rules. What covering angel was set so high by God? Verse 15 concludes with the most definite clue of all by saying: "till iniquity was found in thee."

It is evident that this passage was written about the chief fallen angel. His name is Lucifer. We know him more commonly as Satan. Many are surprised to learn that, prior to his fall, Satan was upheld by God to be the most highly respected and honored of all of God's creation. This is primarily because of the immense responsibility for which he was created. Lucifer's job was to point all creation to God. This was accomplished through worship—a job for which he was well equipped. Later, we will look at how he was equipped. First, let's discuss his fall.

Jesus once told His disciples that He saw Lucifer fall from heaven like lightning. Through the prophet Isaiah, God unveiled Lucifer's plan to exalt himself and to lift his throne above the throne of God. Isaiah 14:12-15 reads:

> How art thou fallen from heaven, O Lucifer, son
> of the morning! How art thou cut down to the
> ground, which didst weaken the nations! For thou
> hast said in thine heart, I will ascend into heaven,

> I will exalt my throne above the stars of God: I will sit also upon the mount of the congregation, in the sides of the north: I will ascend above the heights of the clouds; I will be like the most High. Yet thou shalt be brought down to hell, to the sides of the pit.

Scripture records that Lucifer made a futile attempt to overthrow the throne of God. Met with absolute defeat, Lucifer fell to earth with a fiery vengeance to corrupt all God's creation. The idea that Satan is a distant foe who really doesn't have any dealings with man is altogether wrong. He knows that mankind is the apple of God's eye. However, he has fallen from a very prominent place and now finds himself in total rejection and hopelessness. Satan now watches as mankind possesses the opportunity to rise to the place of acceptance and glory where he once stood. His desire is to see all creation fall to the pit of despair with which he is now faced.

Despite all our grizzly perceptions about the devil, Ezekiel 28:13 describes him as a unique and wonderful creation: "The workmanship of thy tabrets and of thy pipes was prepared in thee in the day that thou wast created." Tabrets and pipes are instruments of worship. These instruments are commonly referred to throughout the Old Testament. There are some Bible translations that leave out these words from this text or even change the language to mean something else. However, they appear in the original language, and I believe it was no mistake. If we take the original writings at face value, it would mean that God equipped Lucifer with built-in musical instruments, or maybe, he simply was an instrument of worship altogether. This is possibly the most telling clue that identifies God's original purpose for Lucifer. Could it be that Lucifer was created to worship and praise God through music and to influence others to do so also? Adorned with precious jewels and gold, he would have been a musical instrument like no other. Regardless of which translation you choose, one thing is certain, Lucifer was an incredible creation who was given remarkable qualities.

The Purpose of Music

When considering this, it makes perfect sense. Music is at the heart of God's creation. In fact, much of the Bible was written in song, and many of the great patriarchs in the Bible were psalmists or poets. The very middle of the Bible contains the largest book—Psalms, a collection of songs. Just as it happened in biblical eras, times of spiritual revival today are also times of musical inspiration and creation. God shows His desire for our musical inspiration to thrive by commanding us to sing a new song unto the Lord. God wants us to verbalize our musical abilities in every new culture and time that emerges. He wants every new generation to experience the newness of His presence and glory through musical worship. It is no wonder the being God originally purposed to bring every new generation into a total worship experience with endless influence and creativity was created as an instrument of worship.

Even though God created music, very few use it for its original purpose. It is, however, a huge part of our everyday life. Music is very influential. Whole generations have been changed by its influence; and that is certainly true of our generation. This change has been both positive and negative and the trend doesn't seem to be slowing.

Satan's Lullaby

Years ago, I learned an interesting way that music changes people. Before my wife and I brought our firstborn child

24

home from the hospital, we were overwhelmed by the seemingly endless supply of child-rearing resources supplied to us by the hospital nursery. Among the material was a collection of lullabies on a cassette tape attached to a booklet. The booklet claimed that babies who were subjected to lullabies were more teachable by the time they reached kindergarten age.

Can a lullaby really have such a great effect? How does this work? Music causes something to happen in the mind. It can excite people or bore them. It can bring happiness, sadness, comfort, or irritation. Almost any emotion that can be experienced can be induced by music. Movie producers understand this concept well. They spend an incredible amount of their budget on music. They know that music can drive the mind to anticipate things that otherwise would seem dull or even unpleasant. In the case of a lullaby, music causes listeners to lose awareness of the world around them, and if successful, it puts them to sleep. The word *lull* implies relaxing the mind and softening the awareness of one's surroundings.

Since his fall, Satan no longer fulfills his intended purpose. He is now using his influence to cause others to fall away as well. Though seemingly detached from reality and even thought by many to be only a religious fairy tale, Satan is extremely busy playing his song. He fully realizes how persuasively powerful he is. Although many think him nonexistent, he is very much alive and active. Metaphorically speaking, he has learned our song. It's a lullaby. We've heard it for so long that we don't even realize it is still being played. Most of the time, Satan isn't trying to destroy our faith with one fell swoop; but with persistence, he sings his song, attempting to lull us into deception. Willing to use any method possible, he searches for ways that fit our personality to separate us from God's presence.

My prayer is that this book will enlighten your understanding about the work of Satan so that you may be equipped to silence Satan's lullaby.

THE SONG

Questions for Thought:

1. What is the general purpose of creation according to Scripture?

2. According to Psalm 100:3, what metaphor is used to describe our relationship with God?

3. For what specific purpose was Lucifer created?

4. How was he equipped to do this job?

5. How does he use his influence and ability today?

6. Why is Satan so jealous of mankind?

Looking Back:
- Understand the original purpose for Lucifer/Satan's creation
- Recount the reasons for Satan's fall.
- Recognize Satan's agenda and why he targets humanity.

Looking Forward:
In the next chapter, we will begin to unveil some ways that Satan targets humanity and also take a look at the tools that he uses to accomplish his goals.

SATAN'S *Lullaby*

CHAPTER 2

THE RIGHT TOOL

"Now the serpent was more subtil than any beast of the field which the Lord God had made" (Genesis 3:1).

I am a believer that if a job is to be done right, then the correct tools should be used. I cringe when I see someone using a knife as a screwdriver. That is asking for an injury and a broken knife. While I concede that improvising sometimes works, using the right tool just makes good sense. When a job becomes a continuous task, it pays to take the time to gather the right tools. Efficiency becomes a key element. Understanding this simple concept, it should come as no surprise that Satan has equipped himself with an array of quality tools. With thousands of years of experience, he has learned which tool works best in almost every situation. When Satan attacks, the right tools will be on the table.

Tools can be used as important instruments of construction or demolition. What God builds, Satan attempts to destroy. Motive and method come into play when determining how a tool is to be used. The word *tool* will be used in this chapter to describe anything or anybody used by Satan in an attempt to impact, control, or destroy. We will also look at numerous passages and illustrations in order to better understand Satan's methodology.

Satan and Job

In the first two chapters of the Book of Job, we find an illustration of how ruthlessly destructive Satan can be. In this passage, there came a day in which all the angels were to present themselves. Satan, also being present, tells God that he had been wandering throughout the world looking for people to destroy. God asked Satan if he had considered Job. Satan reminded God there was no avenue into Job's life. God had provided a hedge of protection around him and everything that belonged to him. The Bible tells us why Job had been afforded this place of security. The Book of Job begins: "There was a man in the land of Uz, whose name was Job; and that man was perfect and upright, and one that feared God, and eschewed evil" (Job 1:1).

This is an incredible witness of a person's life. Very few people will ever have such a testimony attributed to them. Job truly understood the principle of higher living. However, in order to show Satan the determination in Job's heart, God removed the hedge of protection from Job's family, financial security, and even his body. Satan orchestrated an attack against Job. Subsequently, Job lost his children, his wealth, his health, his friends, and seemingly all hope of recovery. In Satan's mind, these were the right tools. In spite of all these things, Satan lost the most important objective in the attack. He could not destroy Job's relationship with God.

Why does God allow us to be tested this way? In Job's case, he was already living a victorious life before Satan entered the picture. So, what is God looking for? Or better yet, what is God trying to show us? In the kingdom of God, tests are not passing or failing; they are passed or taken again. God wants us to understand that testing refines faith, and untested, we can't receive the best God has to offer. The Bible teaches us that we are blessed after we have been tested. When we overcome, then we receive the crown of life.

This is exactly what happened in Job's case. Job was determined that, in spite of what he might experience, he would not curse God as Satan had predicted. God already knew this. That is why he used Job to defeat Satan. Job was a tool in the hands of God. Being used of God can be a very uncomfortable or even painful experience at the time. However, we must remember that the eventual benefit, if we remain faithful, produces a return far greater than the pain we experienced. In return for Job's faithfulness, Job would eventually receive double what had been stolen by Satan.

The Strategies of Satan

God uses our trials as opportunities to overcome Satan and bring blessings into our lives. In the process, however, we find out just how Satan operates. When he attacks, he focuses on the weakest possible places in our lives. He makes it his business to know all about us, studying our habits, our actions, reactions, plans, and desires. He looks for something that we might hold in higher regard than our relationship with God. He finds out what is really important to us. When he sees what he believes to be the most vulnerable place, he then gets personal. He intrudes into our relationships and assaults our security. He uses issues such as health and wealth to weigh us down. He searches out the right tools. Just like we do, Satan learns from trial and error.

After studying our weaknesses and gathering the right tools, he waits for the right time. It is often said not to go to the grocery store on an empty stomach. The empty feeling causes us to jump at anything that will satisfy us. Satan looks for those "empty-stomach" times. When we find ourselves facing desperation, Satan goes to work.

For example, during World War II, Adolf Hitler devised one of the toughest defense plans that this world had ever seen. He built a large wall around the ocean front of German occupied Europe. It became known as the Atlantic Wall. Due to the Atlantic Wall, the success of any invasion depended upon some very important details. First, the invasion had to be made at the weakest part of the wall that could be reached by landing craft. Hitler was so convinced that Allied forces would take the shortest route of invasion that he beefed up that part of the wall with premier strength. In doing so, he left many areas vulnerable that could still be reached by landing craft. To Hitler's surprise, the Allied forces traveled much farther than expected and put in much more effort than he ever thought possible. Second, the timing of the invasion would have to be just right. Even at the weakest places in the wall, there were still insurmountable obstacles on the beach in front of the wall. Putting a landing craft on the beach would be suicidal, unless the tides were just right. When the waterfront receded enough to allow a beach landing where there were no explosive mines, the attack would begin. This event happened only once per moon cycle. The forces waited for just the right moment. Completely avoiding the area that Hitler was convinced would be attacked, the Allied forces captured a beachhead at a small unlikely town called Normandy. This was the action that led the way to the eventual victory in Europe.

Satan uses this same tactic. He goes far out of the way to find weak areas in our lives and then bombards us with overwhelming temptations and struggles. He catches us "when our stomachs are empty"—when we are the most vulnerable. There is no area Satan will not attack if he believes he can breach our defenses. He is constantly searching for new ways into our lives. Although he must operate inside the laws of God's creation, we must still guard our hearts and minds in our weakest areas. James 1:13-14 states, "Let no man say when he is tempted, I am tempted of God: for God cannot be tempted with evil, neither tempteth he any man: But every man is tempted, when he is drawn away of his own lust, and enticed."

Any temptation that Satan brings against us must be related to the feelings that are natural to mankind. God created desires in man to fulfill his own will, but Satan uses these God-given desires by twisting and perverting them. Experiencing desire is not a sin. However, when we allow the devil to use those desires to entice us to do something against God's will, then we become slaves to sin. Because of sin's influence, our very own nature is contrary to God's nature in some way or another. Everyone experiences feelings that lead us away from God's purpose. The part of our nature which is opposite of God's, can be manifested in any number of ways. However, we must remember that our feelings are the last thing that we should trust. There is a belief that if we feel a certain way, then God made us that way. It is easy to forget that we are drawn away by our own lusts and blame our condition on God. God entices no one to sin. Our temptations are the result of our own inner desires; whether our temptation is something we embrace or despise, it can be used by Satan to gain entry into our lives if we allow access.

The real point of reference to determine right and wrong is truth. Truth has no direct correlation with feelings. In fact, our feelings can be driven back and forth by our circumstances or emotions. Feelings are not absolute, but truth is. The theory that absolute truth doesn't exist has severe consequences. If truth doesn't exist, then neither does right and wrong. Mankind would then become a god unto himself by becoming a slave to his own flesh. The end result of this theory leaves Satan armed with a collection of useful tools to bring destruction. Nonetheless, truth does exist. God has given us His Word and confirms it in the lives of those who embrace it.

Building Up Our Walls

Looking back at the Atlantic Wall, another lesson can be learned. Instead of using socialist-minded laborers that would surely pledge themselves to his plan, Hitler used forced labor to build his wall. These slaves dealt the first blow against the wall by allowing intentional weaknesses. When we build our walls against sin, it is important that we pour in our very best.

The Bible gives us a good illustration to consider. In Scripture, the city of Jerusalem can be used to represent the presence of God in our lives. The city was made up of two very important elements from which we can learn. First, there was the Temple, which was God's dwelling place. Second, there were the walls which offered complete protection for the Temple that it surrounded. During the Babylonian conquest in the days of Jeremiah, the walls of Jerusalem were torn down. Many years later, God called Nehemiah to completely rebuild it. This task was met by every obstacle that the enemies of the Jews could conceive. They knew if the walls were completed, then the people of Jerusalem would regain their ability to stand. Because of the opposition, Nehemiah had to commit all his energy and resources to building the wall. His commitment, along with the commitment of the inhabitants of Jerusalem, earned them the ability to regain their freedom.

Like the enemies of the Jews in this story, Satan also wants our walls in a state of ruin. He knows that if we build our defenses against him, he has no way to destroy God's dwelling place in our hearts. For this reason, Satan brings obstacles into our lives. The key to building and keeping our defenses strong is in James 4:7: "Resist the devil, and he will flee from you."

Here, the word *resist* has the same meaning as in the phrase "resisting arrest." God gives us enough strength to resist and escape every temptation that comes into our lives. This is not always easy. To resist Satan, we must first draw close to God. In His presence, we find strength beyond our own ability. To draw close to God, we must approach him with a heart of true repentance. When we do, God opens the door to His presence. Only then do we find the resources to withstand the most incredible attacks of Satan.

The Tool of Satan—Lies

There is yet another lesson we can learn from the illustration about Hitler's strategies. Long before the first shot was fired against Poland, Hitler began a different type of warfare called *propaganda*. Propaganda is simple—tell lies loud enough and long enough until the lie is believed. The soldier in this warfare isn't armed with physical weapons. His stockpile is filled with agendas and lies. Hitler bolstered so much support for the socialist movement that he was able to overtake five countries without firing a single shot. They simply allowed his takeover. This wasn't a quick battle. It took years to break down loyalty to people's homelands, but when the change of heart came, Hitler was ready. This is a clear picture of how our Enemy works. Satan isn't just a liar; he is the father of all lies. He tells just enough truth to get our attention and just enough lies to separate us from God. John 8:32 shows us the way to steer clear of those lies—"The truth shall make you free."

This promise can only benefit those who have knowledge of the truth. The beacon that serves as the point of reference for all people is God's Word. It is the only source for absolute truth. When we don't know or don't believe God's Word, we have obvious weaknesses, and Satan knows how to exploit them. All he needs is the right tool. To see this illustrated, all we have to do is look at the very first act of disobedience ever recorded. The story begins in Genesis 3:1. It reads: "Now the serpent was more subtil than any beast of the field which the Lord God had made."

Following this verse, is the story about how Satan used the serpent to betray mankind into sin. There are two important things to know about the context of this story. First, God had placed man over all the animals, including the serpent.

Second, before the fall of man, there was no fear between different kinds of species or between species and man. In fact, Adam and Eve lived among all species with no problems. When choosing a route to man, Satan naturally used the most cunning of all animals—the serpent. Today, when we think of snakes, we want them as far away as possible. During that day, however, the snake had the subtle ability to exist close to man without causing any fear or concern. No tool could be better utilized by Satan to convince them of his lies. Either by taking on the form of a serpent or simply possessing a serpent, Satan began a conversation with Eve. In Genesis 3:1, Satan questions Eve, "Yea hath God said, Ye shall not eat of every tree of the garden?"

At this point, it was vital that Eve understood God's will. Satan implemented the tactic of using only a portion of God's words with them. This same tactic is still used today. It is surprising how little emphasis is placed on the study and learning of God's Word. At best, the average Christian has only a basic understanding of the tenets that define a particular faction of faith. Because of this, false doctrine prospers throughout the world. Had Eve been unfamiliar with God's Word, she would have been defenseless against this strategy. The same holds true for anyone who encounters Satan. Instead of succumbing to this tactic, she finished the statement that Satan began by saying: "We may eat of the fruit of the trees of the garden, but of the tree which is in the midst of the garden, God hath said, ye shall not eat of it, neither shall ye touch it, lest ye die" (Gen. 3:2-3).

The serpent replied, "Ye shall not surely die" (v. 4).

How many times has Satan denied the certainty of God's Word? One of the most dangerous lies that Satan continues to tell is that transgressing the commandment of God bears no consequence. In Isaiah 28:15, Isaiah describes the false belief of the wayward priest of his day. In a drunken state, the priests and even prophets declared: "We have made a covenant with death, and with hell are we at agreement; when the overflowing scourge shall pass through, it shall not come unto us: for we have made lies our refuge, and under falsehood have we hid ourselves."

Even in their degenerate condition, the priests and prophets of that day had convinced themselves that they had become exempt from God's wrath. However, God's reply in verse 18 was, "Your covenant with death shall be disannulled, and your agreement with hell shall not stand; when the overflowing scourge shall pass through, then ye shall be trodden down by it."

God has made it clear where He stands on this issue; sin brings judgment. Remember the serpent's response, "Ye shall not surely die." What a lie. At the very moment Adam and Eve disobeyed God, they were contaminated with a disease called sin. This separated them from God's presence and ensured certain death. We must keep in mind that the same thing that separated mankind from God in the beginning has the ability to separate mankind from him today. Sin has no place in the heart of a believer.

Reading on, we discover the blow that drove the lie home was a misplaced truth. Genesis 3:5 says, "For God doth know that in the day ye eat thereof, then your eyes shall be opened, and ye shall be as gods, knowing good and evil."

Satan was implying that God was holding back the very best. He made something forbidden to mankind seem essential to them. However, what Adam and Eve really gained in the day that sin entered was shame. Shame accompanies sin. Verse 6 describes Eve's actions that brought her into sin: "And when the woman saw that the tree was good for food, and that it was pleasant to the eyes, and a tree to be desired to make one wise, she took of the fruit thereof."

The words good, pleasant, and desired all appear in this one statement. Notice that Satan turns Eve's attention to the desirable qualities of the forbidden. Satan never glorifies the goodness of the things allowed by God. We sometimes forget how blessed we are. We live in a modern world of innovation and luxury, but we are more discontent than ever. It seems as if life has become all about searching for and having better things.

Giving Away Our Birthright

Several years ago, my wife and I began to search for a larger home. This became an all-consuming project. After looking at many houses, we finally found the one that felt right. That night, as we were driving back into the driveway of the house in which we were living, something strange happened to both of us at about the same time. It became obvious to us that there was no reason for us to move. We liked our home, and finding a nicer one wasn't really going to change much. We wondered why we began searching in the first place.

Solomon tells us in the Book of Ecclesiastes that the heart of man can never be satisfied with carnal things. It doesn't matter how much we have, we always want more. How easy it is for Satan to use this. The Garden of Eden was full of good trees and fruit, but Satan caused man to focus on the one and only thing that God did not allow.

What is it that causes mankind to choose inferiority on the road to excellence? God has great plans for humanity. Sadly, most people will never reach the maximum potential of God's perfect will—instead they choose a quick and fleeting reward in exchange for His wonderful blessing. Eve had the honor of being the mother of all living, but more important, she had the divine right to walk with God in the Garden. She sacrificed all of it for one moment of desire.

Many people throughout Scripture have made similar mistakes. A good example is Esau selling his birthright. Esau had a twin brother who was born moments after him. Being the oldest son, Esau was the heir to his father's fortune, but Esau's brother Jacob was bent on turning the tables. One day, while Esau was out hunting, he became fatigued and hungry. He found himself "hungry in the grocery store." Jacob saw Esau's moment of desperation and took advantage of him. Esau sold his birthright to Jacob for a bowl of beans. Sounds crazy doesn't it? The truth is, everywhere we look, people are selling their birthrights for a moment of temporary satisfaction.

We all face desperation at some point. When we do, Satan attempts to use these moments as leverage points against us, but God offers strength in His presence. Hebrews 4:16 instructs us to "come boldly unto the throne of grace, that we may obtain mercy, and find grace to help in time of need."

This ability to rely on God's mercy and grace for strength allows us as believers to remain victorious. As we move farther on, we will learn more of how to take advantage of this wonderful privilege, but for now, let's continue uncovering Satan's strategy.

Questions for Thought:

1. Why does God allow us to be tested?

2. Is being used by God always a comfortable experience? Why?

3. What benefits can we receive by facing spiritual tests?

4. What are some of the specific things about us that Satan studies?

5. What are some of the strategies that Satan uses to attack us?

6. Why does Satan want our "walls" in a state of ruin?

7. What gives us the ability to overcome the attacks of Satan?

Looking Back:
- Know the tools Satan uses to attempt to destroy us.
- Understand the cruelty and ruthlessness of Satan's attacks.
- Recognize the main strategies of Satan's attacks.

Looking Forward:
In the next chapter, we will explore Satan's greatest strategy to gain a foothold in our lives.

SATAN'S *Lullaby*

CHAPTER 3

FIGHTING SLEEP

"And she made him sleep upon her knees" (Judges 16:19).

A mother I know once told me about her daughter who, as an infant, used to fight sleep horribly. She tried music, car rides, mobiles, rocking chairs, and an array of other ideas to help her baby to fall asleep. Nothing worked. One night she stumbled upon a much-needed discovery. Not able to sleep, she decided to wash clothes. To put the clothes into the dryer, she laid her child on a blanket that she had placed on top of the dryer. Just as soon as the dryer started, the child began to relax and then to sleep. It worked every time after that. Imagine taking your child to the dryer instead of to the crib when it is time to go "night-night."

Making a child fall asleep can be very tricky. I once had quite an experience with this. Several years ago, my daughter was determined to have her ears pierced. Being so young, she didn't fully grasp the fact that a piece of metal would be forced through her earlobe. After every effort to convince her to wait a few more years, we finally gave in to her persistent begging. We took her to the piercing center at the local superstore. I will never forget the smile on her face as that long-awaited moment finally arrived. She hopped into

43

the chair with anticipation. Without any fear, she positioned herself for what turned out to be the surprise of her four-year-old life. When the clerk pulled the trigger on the piercing gun, she immediately gained the attention of the entire store with a dramatic scream. Refusing to let the other ear be pierced, we went home with one pierced ear.

For the next few days, we tried every conceivable way to bribe her into returning to the piercing center to finish the job, but she was satisfied with one pierced ear. We finally resorted to buying a self-piercing kit. It goes without saying that I was not looking forward to piercing my daughter's other ear, but a dad has to do what a dad has to do. I thought it would be best if we waited for her to fall asleep. The moment finally came. I put the device onto her ear, but before I could muster up the courage to pull the trigger, she woke up realizing exactly what was about to happen. In a panic, she jumped up and escaped. From then on it was a waiting game. All I had to do was wait for her to fall back asleep, but suddenly she had the stamina to remain awake all night. She knew that if I fell asleep first, then I couldn't pierce her other ear. I was determined to outlast her, but she fought sleep like a champion, thus proving to daddy that she couldn't be beat. After that night, I couldn't make myself try again, but a few years later, a braver little girl returned to the piercing center and got both of her ears pierced.

The Dangers of Drowsiness and Distraction

While we can laugh about such stories, there is a dark spiritual parallel to this idea. For Satan to be able to complete his work, he must catch believers in a state of spiritual slumber. First Peter 5:8 warns, "Be sober, be vigilant; because your adversary the devil, as a roaring lion, walketh about, seeking whom he may devour."

A few years back, a missionary to Africa told me about the hunting habits of lions. He told me that deer are one of their favorite foods. In Africa, deer travel in herds to protect themselves from lions. Instead of attacking the herd, lions look for an isolated victim. I was fascinated to learn one of the more common reasons that deer fall away from the herd. Even though deer usually remain in constant awareness of their surroundings, they can't seem to avoid the temptation to stare at ants. Their curiosity is so overwhelming that they sometimes lose total awareness of everything else and stare at ants until the herd has moved on. Once the herd is gone, their security is gone. Soon they realize that they are the single object of a group of hungry lions. Because they lose their focus, they lose their life.

There are also little things in our lives that have the potential to distract us and cause us to drift away from our source of security. Our source of security as Christians is found in the center of God's presence. In order to separate us from that place, Satan will try just about anything to lull us into a state of spiritual slumber. We've all heard the story about the hare and the tortoise. The tortoise didn't stand a chance of winning a race with the hare—until the hare fell asleep. The same is true in our lives. We have the advantage over Satan as long as we remain spiritually awake, but just as ants can cause deer to lose focus, so can little things cause us to fall spiritually asleep. For this reason, Satan digs down and stirs up spiritual ants. First John 2:15-17 instructs us to "Love not the world, neither the things that are in the world. If any man love the world, the love of the Father is not in him. For all that is in the world, the lust of the flesh, and the lust of the eyes, and the pride of life, is not of the Father, but is of the world. And the world passeth away, and the lust thereof: but he that doeth the will of God abideth for ever."

It is evident that we live in this world, but a Christian is not of the world. The social order of a Christian comes from above and is a reflection of God's will. The Scripture tells us that those who do the will of God shall abide forever. The ants in our lives are the things that separate us from God's will. John places these things into three categories: "the lust of the eyes, the lust of the flesh, and the pride of life." Twisting the desires of man, Satan uses them as weapons against us.

Samson's Lullaby

This concept is illustrated in the Book of Judges in chapters 13–16. Samson is a man who stands far apart from all the other champions of the Bible. Reading the story of his life can be like reading the story of a comic book superhero, except he actually did exist. A common scenario seemed to recur throughout his life. He repeatedly found himself trapped in impossible situations. Inevitably, the power of God would come upon him, and he would accomplish some superhuman act to save the day. This ability that evidenced itself this way was a gift from God intended to bring deliverance to the Israelites who were being oppressed by the Philistines. To the Philistines, he seemed invincible, but Samson had one notable weakness—he couldn't resist the appeal of a beautiful woman. In pursuit of his lust, he began misusing the anointing that was upon his life. Anything upon which he laid his eyes would become his, or someone would pay a terrible price. Because of this, the only thing that came of Samson's dealings with the Philistines was a greater hatred and persecution of Israel. That which had been intended to be a blessing for Israel only brought further suffering. Amazingly, God's anointing remained with him through this time of personal weakness.

God never removed this gift from Samson as long as he didn't reveal the secret of his strength. Because of a vow upon his life, Samson believed that cutting his hair would cause his strength to leave. If he were to reveal this belief, he would be in violation of his conscience. To him, keeping this secret meant pleasing God. The Bible teaches us that anything that is not of faith is sin. As long as Samson maintained his secret, he was within the margins of his own conscience.

Knowing that Samson's most notable weakness was his lust for women, the Philistines hired the one person Samson cherished most of all to find out the secret of his strength. Her name was Delilah. No doubt, she was a very attractive woman. The Philistines offered her a great sum to "crack the code" that revealed the source of his strength. Using her God-given natural beauty in a very ungodly way, she began to wear down the spiritual strength of Samson. From the moment that Delilah began searching for the secret of his strength, he should have removed himself from her presence. However, his desire was strong, and his spirit had grown weary. Having been lulled into a state of spiritual slumber, he finally revealed his secret.

This story is an incredible example for us. Christ taught that if our strong hand or good eye brings us offense, that we should remove them. Jesus wasn't suggesting that we dismember our bodies, but instead, He was asking us to separate ourselves from those things that might cause us to surrender to sin. Romans 13:14 says, "Make not provision for the flesh, to fulfil the lusts thereof."

All of us have areas of potential weakness. It is very important that we identify these areas. If we are not intentional about guarding these places in our lives, then we allow these things to become weapons in the hands of the Enemy. That is exactly what happened to Samson. Because Samson let down his guard, Satan preyed upon his personal weakness, thus bringing Samson into both spiritual and physical bondage.

The focal verse of this chapter was the key to Satan's victory over Samson. Judges 16:19 tells us that Delilah caused Samson to fall asleep on her lap. She didn't use force or some drug. She began to relax and comfort him until he was lulled into a deep sleep. She became his best friend only to become his worst enemy. Samson's proximity to this wayward woman was a clear indicator of his spiritual state. Samson didn't fail because he fell asleep physically; he failed because he fell asleep spiritually. Samson had allowed Satan to position obstacles in his life that he would not be able to continually overcome. This is how Satan works. He looks for ways to get close and personal in our lives. If possible, he uses those who are closest to us. Once Samson fell asleep, the Philistines shaved his head. When Delilah woke him, just like the deer at the beginning of this chapter, he found himself the single object of a group of hungry lions. The Philistines had surrounded him at his time of spiritual isolation.

What followed was devastating. The Bible says he didn't know that the Lord had departed from him. For the first time in his life, he found that the power of God was not simply at his disposal. It had only been available to him because the presence of God had been with him. Samson failed to guard the one thing he believed was key to maintaining God's favor. As a result, he paid a terrible price.

When God removes His favor from someone, destruction is sure to follow. This doesn't mean that everyone who experiences hardship is out of God's favor. What it does mean is that when God's favor is gone, destruction will eventually be the result. For this reason, it is crucial that we guard the things that bring God's favor into our lives. The way we do this is by living with a good conscience in the eyes of God, working to please Him in everything.

It took Samson losing his strength, being captured and tortured by the enemy, and having his eyes put out to realize the magnitude of living outside of God's favor. This realization led Samson to the spiritual place where he would finally accomplish the feat for which he was born. In a sincere moment of repentance, Samson begged for the favor of God on his life once more. Because of true repentance, God honored his prayer. With renewed strength, he was able to push the pillars out from under the building where all of the leaders of the Philistines were gathered. As a result, he lost his own life, but the Bible explains that more Philistines were destroyed in Samson's death than in all of his life's efforts, thus delivering Israel from the oppression of the Philistines.

An important lesson is learned here. When our gifts are directed by the will of God, more can be accomplished in that moment than in all of our self-willed efforts combined. Our efforts are multiplied by His favor.

Equipped for the Battle

If you carefully read through the biblical account of Samson, you will find a common thread—out of death comes life. You will find that he once ate honey from a dead lion. In another place, he brought about a great victory using the jawbone of a dead donkey as a weapon, and through Samson's death, the will of God was accomplished. The New Testament speaks of the change in the nature of a believer by saying, "Old things are passed away; behold, all things are become new" (2 Corinthians 5:17).

We can only experience the best of what God has in store for us when we, as Christians, allow the person that we once were to die. Our new identity is modeled after a life of holiness, and a life of holiness leads to a life filled with God's anointing. This is why Satan wants to remove us from God's presence. He knows that a Christian in the center of God's will has enough strength to ward off any spiritual attack. Jesus told Simon Peter: "Upon this rock I will build my church, and the gates of hell shall not prevail against it" (Matthew 16:18). This passage depicts the domain of Satan under attack by the forces of the church. The church, in large, doesn't understand its divine privilege. God has given us the ability to render Satan's power useless when we stand in His favor.

I once read about a soldier in the 101st Airborne Division during the invasion at Normandy. He was armed with a device that could melt the inner components of machine guns. When finding an unmanned bunker, he would destroy the weapons inside. Upon the return of the opposing forces, they would discover that they had lost their ability to fight. Similarly, God allows us to render Satan's weapons useless. Second Corinthians 10:4 says, "For the weapons of our warfare are not carnal, but mighty through God to the pulling down of strong holds."

God equips Christians who are in the center of His will with the ability to reach beyond the natural things that surround them. Instead, they are able to target the command post of the spiritual attack. That is where Satan stands as the commanding officer. When we walk in obedience to God, the weapons of our warfare are truly more than mighty enough through God to destroy the strongholds of the Enemy. Paul warned the church at Ephesus that it was not enemies of flesh and blood they fought, but rather spiritual forces that would prey upon their carnal weaknesses (see Ephesians 6:12). This is probably the best way to describe an attack of Satan. When we shore up our weak spots, we render Satan's weapons useless. Without a way to break into our life, he is powerless to bring spiritual destruction. A stronghold of

Satan is nothing more than a spiritual weakness related to a carnal tendency. This is why we must remain on guard, never falling into spiritual slumber.

Staying Alert

The night before Jesus was crucified, he told His disciples to "Watch and pray, that ye enter not into temptation: the spirit indeed is willing, but the flesh is weak" (Matthew 26:41). The word *watch* in this passage simply means to stay awake. Jesus saw the potential for the disciples to let down their guard spiritually. He knew of the coming battle the disciples would face, but they did not heed His warning. At the greatest time of trial, the disciples deserted their Teacher, falling hard to the onslaught of the Enemy. However, in time, God restored them to the place of spiritual strength. Their battle with Satan stood as a hard reminder that they must remain vigilant at all times.

At the beginning of this chapter, I recounted a story about my daughter fighting sleep to stay awake longer than me. As long as she remained awake, I couldn't pierce her ear. Just the same, our spirit must outlast our flesh. In the Book of Judges, Samson learned this the hard way. He ended up losing the very thing that brought him down. The Philistines gouged out his eyes. After that moment, he began to see things more clearly than ever before, but this time, from the right perspective. When God allowed Samson's demise, it turned out to be the greatest act of grace that Samson had ever received. God taught him what it really took to remain victorious. Samson preceded his final work with prayer. In a single action, he accomplished the feat for which he was born. What a difference the power of God makes in a person's life. When we remain awake spiritually, God can do the same thing in our lives.

Questions for Thought:

1. Where is the source of security for a Christian found?

2. According to 1 John 2:17, who shall abide forever?

3. Anything that is not of faith is _____.

4. We all have spiritual weaknesses. What do you need to guard against in your own life?

5. What eventually happens to a person from whom God removes His favor?

6. Why did God honor Samson's final request?

7. What happens when our God-given anointing is directed toward accomplishing God's will?

8. How can you stay in the "center of God's will" so that you may ward off the attacks of Satan?

Looking Back:

- Understand the importance of remaining spiritually awake.
- Be aware that Satan's greatest strategy is to stir up distractions to lull us into spiritual slumber.
- Know the importance of staying in the center of God's will so that you may ward off the attacks of Satan.

Looking Forward:

In the next chapter, we will discover how to find a safe place from Satan's attack on our lives.

CHAPTER 4

THE DWELLING PLACE

"He that dwelleth in the secret place of the
most High shall abide under the shadow of the
Almighty" (Psalm 91:1).

A t first, this book may give the impression that we must
live our lives in a slugfest with the devil. Even though
he would like us to think so, that simply isn't true. There is a
place of refuge we can go to where God will fight our battles
for us. For obvious reasons, Satan doesn't want us there, but
it is a wonderful place to be. On two occasions in Scripture,
God can be found speaking through a prophet, instructing
the people of God to stand still and see the salvation of the
Lord. In both cases, the people were in a very tough place;
and in both cases, God performed an incredible miracle. In-
terestingly, there are a number of times when even the arch-
angels admonished Satan simply by saying, "the Lord re-
bukes you." When God speaks, Satan must obey. This gives
credence to Paul's observation that "if God be for us, who
can be against us?" (Romans 8:31).

So, how do we get to the place where God fights our
battles for us? We have seen several examples so far of what
comes when we find ourselves outside the will of God. Now,
let's examine what is available to us when we are in His
perfect will.

A Blessing Instead of a Curse

In Numbers 22, we find the record of Israel's first encounter with the kingdom of Moab. At this point in history, Moab was a puppet kingdom of the mighty Amorites, as found in Numbers 21:29. Soon after destroying the Amorites, the children of Israel were now situated just outside of Moab. The ease with which Israel overcame the Amorites struck overwhelming fear in the hearts of the people of Moab. Hoping to defeat Israel without military strength, Balak, the king of Moab hired the prophet Balaam to speak a curse against Israel. Balaam's accuracy of foretelling events was so stunning that Balak, the king of Moab, believed that if Balaam spoke a prophecy, it would have to come to pass. Balak offered Balaam a large reward to speak a curse against Israel, but Balaam knew all he could do was speak; it was up to God to bring a curse. Balaam didn't hide this fact, but made clear that he would speak only the words that God put in his mouth. Still, Balak continued with his plan.

Like many today, Balak thought that by seeking spiritual advice, he could take charge of his own future. He made a very expensive sacrifice and then took Balaam to the high places of the false god, Baal. From this vantage point, the plains of Moab could be seen. He was, in his mind, stacking the deck. However, the Bible tells us that God met Balaam there. Instead of a curse, God put a blessing in his mouth. This whole process was repeated in a different location with the same outcome. By this time, Balak was infuriated. Balaam began to see his hope of receiving a reward dwindle. Numbers 24:1 says, "And when Balaam saw that it pleased the Lord to bless Israel, he went not, as at other times, to seek for enchantments, but he set his face toward the wilderness."

For a person who had been so incredibly moved by God's anointing in times past, this was an unspeakable fall.

Balaam, a prophet of God, was trying to escape the presence of God in an attempt to avoid divine inspiration. He would later find out the cost of standing in such contradiction to God's position. In spite of his tenacious effort, he couldn't elude God's purpose. The following verse reads, "And Balaam lifted up his eyes, and he saw Israel abiding in his tents according to his tribes; and the spirit of the Lord came upon him" (24:2).

What Balaam saw in the wilderness was breathtaking. In accordance with the tribal arrangements laid out in Numbers 2, three of the 12 tribes of Israel encamped on each of the four sides of the Tabernacle. According to the census recorded in that same chapter, this would cause the encampment to take on the appearance of a cross. Beholding this marvelous vision, the Spirit of God moved upon him to speak one of the most profound utterances ever given about the nation of Israel.

> How goodly are thy tents, O Jacob, and thy tabernacles, O Israel! As the valleys are they spread forth, as gardens by the river's side, as the trees of lign aloes which the LORD hath planted, and as cedar trees beside the waters. He shall pour the water out of his buckets, and his seed shall be in many waters, and his king shall be higher than Agag, and his kingdom shall be exalted. God brought him forth out of Egypt; he hath as it were the strength of an unicorn: he shall eat up the nations his enemies, and shall break their bones, and pierce them through with his arrows. He crouched, he lay down as a lion, and as a great lion: who shall stir him up? Blessed is he that blesseth thee, and cursed is he that curseth thee (Numbers 24:5-9).

In all, no curse could be spoken over the nation of Israel.

It is interesting to note that while all this was taking place, Scripture gives no indication that Israel knew any of this was happening. I asked the question earlier, "How do we get to the place where God fights our battles for us?" The truth is, we may already be there and not know it. Satan wants to sift us as wheat, so why doesn't he? The answer is, he can't operate outside of the parameters that God allows him.

A Place of Refuge

We all experience a measure of grace in our lives. Without it, Satan would immediately pulverize us, but what is it that causes grace to spill over into other parts of our lives so that God's special favor becomes obvious? Psalm 91:1 gives an indication: "He that dwelleth in the secret place of the most High shall abide under the shadow of the Almighty." In modern terms, the phrase *secret place* means a hiding place. This indicates that there is a refuge in God. This passage makes it clear that only those who dwell in the secret place can obtain this favor. Farther on in the chapter we read, "Because thou hast made the Lord, which is my refuge, even the most High, thy habitation; There shall no evil befall thee, neither shall any plague come nigh thy dwelling" (91:9-10).

As in many psalms, point of view can change before the song ends. This is the case with Psalm 91. By the end of the chapter, we find God himself speaking. He talks about those who receive the pronounced blessing of this Psalm. In verse 14, He tells us why He extends this blessing. God says, "Because he hath set his love upon me, therefore will I deliver him."

Love isn't an emotion as most people think. Love is a choice and can be proven by our actions. God's nature is to love, and He does it unconditionally. When we place conditions upon our love, we are really only serving ourselves and not loving others. True love doesn't look inward to serve itself—true love looks outward. It isn't about what we feel; it's a choice we make. Love is selfless. Only by loving God can we dwell in the secret place. There are a number of actions that could prove or disprove our love for God. There are more than could be discussed in a single book. However, if we sincerely examine our actions and motives, we know whether or not we are really loving God or serving ourselves.

In John 14:15, Jesus told His disciples, "If ye love me, keep my commandments." Sin is the breaking of God's commandments. By abstaining from sin, God promises divine refuge for us. This is what it means to dwell in the secret place. You might have heard someone say that God cannot dwell where sin abounds. The reason for this is because God's nature is holiness. That is why it is so important to Satan to bring sin into the lives of believers. Sin empowers Satan in our lives, but he has no power where there is no sin.

Most of Psalm 91 describes to us an ongoing attack against us. Dwelling in the secret place doesn't stop the attack against our lives; it does however, keep us safe during the attack. Some people have the impression that if they are good enough that bad things will not come their way. This is not at all what the Bible teaches. Looking through the Bible, the argument can easily be built that a prescribed measure of "the attack" is a healthy part of our daily spiritual development. Through exposure to the Enemy's onslaught, not only does God keep us in check, but we also discover God's supreme authority and superiority over all creation. It becomes a faith-building experience. We don't just dwell in some random hiding place, but in "the secret place of the Most High." The things in life that normally strike fear into the heart of believers pale in comparison to the shadow of God when we dwell in His hiding place.

The key to understanding this concept is perception. A few years back, a trainer at a fire academy explained to me the most intense training exercise that a fireman would have to go through. It was called the tower. In this multistory concrete structure were numerous obstacles that a fireman might later encounter on the job. This training exercise was so realistic that trainees would find themselves trapped in burning rooms with no visibility and no apparent way out. There were some who reached such a point of despair that they would literally give up and sit down to die. What they couldn't see was a trainer within arm's reach wearing thermal imaging goggles ready to rescue them when all of their training was forgotten.

We sometimes feel like those trainees felt in the tower. We find ourselves facing impossible situations, believing we are alone. We may even be faced with the possibility of death. What God wants us to see is when we walk in tough places He is always there. In the twenty-third Psalm, David says, "though I walk through the valley of the shadow of death, I will fear no evil: for thou art with me" (v. 4).

Just because we are in a place where Satan has no power doesn't mean that we won't see him at work. The reason he has no power is because when he attacks, God fights for us. Isaiah 59:19 says: "When the enemy shall come in like a flood, the Spirit of the Lord shall lift up a standard against him." A standard is another name for the flag that a soldier carries into battle bearing the seal of a nation or kingdom. What this verse is telling us is that when the Enemy comes picking a fight, the Lord goes to war on our behalf.

This all sounds great, but there is a flipside. If we stopped here, we wouldn't see how this principle also works in reverse. Soon we find our story taking a hard turn. Balaam never forgot about the reward offered by the king. Being a prophet, he understood why Israel had been blessed. In Numbers 23:21, Balaam explained that God had not found iniquity in Israel. He knew that if the people of Israel were going to be cursed, then they would have to invite the curse upon themselves through sin. In pursuit of the king's reward, Balaam devised a plan to bring strong temptation into the camp of Israel. Jesus himself alluded to this event in Revelation 2:14 when he said, "Balaam... taught Balac to cast a stumbling block before the children of Israel, to eat things sacrificed unto idols, and to commit fornication."

A *stumbling block* can be defined as a "hurdle or an obstacle." It doesn't ensure certain failure, but it does cause the target person or group to take evasive action to stay on course. In Numbers 25, just after Balak's failed plan to unjustly curse Israel, we find the people of Israel succumbing to the prostitutes of Moab and worshiping their false god. Balaam had explained to Balak that the practices of the idolatrous daughters of Moab might pull the people of Israel into sin. This is found in Numbers 31:16. God had placed the destiny of Israel into their own hands, but now they were throwing it away. Israel knew the nature of God is holiness. This sin was in obvious defiance of God.

Earlier in the wilderness wandering, God had given the people of Israel the incredible opportunity to experience His presence in the magnificence of His glory. This happened just after the Red Sea crossing at Mount Horeb. God knew this experience would provide the strength and encouragement needed to move forward into the promises He had given them. However, they were afraid to draw near to His presence. Compelling Moses to intercede with God on their behalf, they stood at what they thought was a safe distance. This would prove to be very costly. Had they been armed with a better perspective of the nearness of God, they might

SATAN'S *Lullaby*

not have fallen to the temptation found here in Numbers 25. The writer of Proverbs tells us that a people without a revelation will cast off restraint, and that is exactly what Israel did. Moab sent their daughters to infiltrate the camp of Israel, and the people of Israel quickly abandoned their convictions with abominable actions. For this, they would soon experience the severity of God. The very hand that had been their refuge was now their destroyer. God sent a plague against Israel, which killed twenty-four thousand people. Make no mistake; God despises sin.

This Bible story is one of the most revealing of its kind, which shows Satan's only real method of destroying someone's spiritual life. He has no authority to separate us from God's presence. The only way we can be defeated is if we step outside the dwelling place. This means victory and defeat are not in the hands of Satan, but are in our own hands. Still, Satan faithfully sings his song hoping to find willing victims. By neglecting God's perfect will, they empower Satan to destroy their spiritual lives. A person within God's perfect will grows stronger as a result of Satan's attack. For this reason, God allows Satan just enough leeway to benefit the body of Christ, but not enough leeway to destroy us while walking in obedience.

What we learn from the people of Israel in this story is, choosing a life of sin leads to destruction, and choosing a life above sin carries us into God's dwelling place. Only when we lean on the hand of the one who created us can we live above sin. Our love and passion for God will keep us at that place. After the events of this story, Israel eventually regained their posture, but they learned an important lesson. "He that dwelleth in the secret place of the most High shall abide under the shadow of the Almighty."

60

Questions for Thought:

1. Why won't God dwell where sin abounds?

2. In Psalms 91, what does the phrase *secret place* mean?

3. How does sin empower Satan in our lives?

4. How does dwelling in the secret place of the Most High offer us refuge from the spiritual destruction of Satan?

5. Define *stumbling block*.

6. Does a stumbling block ensure certain failure?

Looking Back:
- Understand that we can find spiritual refuge in God.
- Know the ways we can stay in God's hiding place.
- Be aware of the consequences of stepping away from God and His refuge.

Looking Forward:

In the next chapter, we will discuss sin and its consequences for mankind.

SATAN'S *Lullaby*

PART TWO

Sin and Death

CHAPTER 5

WHEN SIN IS FINISHED

"When lust hath conceived, it bringeth forth sin:
and sin, when it is finished, bringeth forth death"
(James 1:15).

Sin is a willful transgression of God's law or a failure to do what is known to be right. The Bible goes so far as to say that anything that is not of faith is sin. There is much more to sin than what a person may think. Rooted in pride and watered by deception, it takes hold of any who behold it and infects all who conceive it. Its cost is great, and its effect and consequences are eternal.

The first time the word *sin* appears in the Bible is in Genesis 4:7. In this scripture, God is speaking to a man named Cain about doing what is right. Cain's brother Abel brought a sacrifice to God which was accepted, but Cain brought a sacrifice to God which was rejected. Abel's sacrifice was a picture of faith, because it was a blood sacrifice. This painted a picture of the cost of sin. Cain's sacrifice was wrought with his labor, implying that he was trying to earn salvation, which is unachievable. In this passage, God tells Cain:

"If thou doest well, shalt thou not be accepted? And if thou doest not well, sin lieth at the door."

Notice two things about this passage. First, the passage states that he will be accepted if he does well. Galatians 6:9 says, "Let us not be weary in well doing: for in due season we shall reap, if we faint not." This reinforces the Epistle of James when he explains that faith without works is dead. Cain certainly worked, but not according to genuine faith. The type of work Cain did showed faith in his own efforts, but the type of sacrifice Abel made showed faith in God. In response to God's reply, Cain looked outward instead of inward to find the root of his problem. Envy against his brother was born in Cain's heart. His envy became so strong, Cain killed his brother Abel. Because of this, he would bear a curse throughout the rest of his life.

Second, the passage states if he does not do well, "sin lieth at the door." Here, the word sin is personified. It "lieth" at the door. The word *lieth*, in this passage, comes from the Hebrew word *rabats*, which means to crouch like an animal. In other words, sin is ready to pounce.

The Wages of Sin

Paul wrote in Romans 7:11, "For sin, taking occasion by the commandment, deceived me, and by it slew me." Sin kills! Romans 6:23 explains about sin bringing death. This chapter will explain how this principle works.

It is important to know that God does not want anyone to perish in sin. In fact, the entire theme of the Bible is the redemption of mankind. God has gone to incredible measures to redeem us from our sin. That is why we have the *gospel*—the good news. Understanding the process of how sin breaks down our relationship with God is crucial. It is also imperative to look at how obedience builds up our defenses and keeps us in right relationship with God.

The Struggle Against Temptation and Sin

"Blessed is the man that endureth temptation: for when he is tried, he shall receive the crown of life, which the Lord hath promised to them that love him" (James 1:12). This scripture highlights the benefit of enduring temptation. Before the first sin, however, there was no desire to commit offenses against God. After Adam's first sin, a struggle was created for all Adam's descendants. It travels through the seed of man and is passed on to every new generation. Sinful man brings forth sinful man. Since that time, temptation has taken hold of the nature of mankind. Temptation now stands as a hurdle which mankind must cross in order to receive the crown of life. Thus, the response to temptation gauges the true relationship between God and a person.

Jesus told a rich young ruler he lacked just one thing to be saved. That is all it takes. Just one thing which we refuse to relinquish can cause us to miss heaven. Before you close this book in discouragement or disgust, please be encouraged about the power of God which works on our behalf. Jude dedicated his letter in the New Testament to "him that is able to keep you from falling, and to present you faultless" (Jude 24). I once heard a minister speak of those who have enough faith to believe God can deliver them from the penalty of sin, but not the power of sin. Believing God is unable to deliver us from the power of sin cuts short the redemptive work of Christ. Christ gives us the strength to overcome; and in those moments when we do fail, Christ has provided us a way for repentance. Therefore, as long as we live, we are never without the hope of salvation.

Judas Iscariot was a man Jesus personally chose to be a disciple. Jesus knew and understood his heart and soul. When we think of Judas today, it is easy to think of him as being pure evil; but he was just a man. The real problem with

Judas was he had a temptation he would never fully overcome—the lust for money. Jesus knew this, but made Judas the treasurer of His ministry anyway. In John 12, a woman poured out a costly ointment on Jesus. Judas complained that the ointment could have been sold and the money distributed to the poor. Verse six explains the real reason he was upset was because he hoped the money would go into the ministry coffers so he could steal it. Was Jesus being unfair to Judas by making him the treasurer? Shouldn't Jesus have understood that Judas couldn't resist? The answer is no. Jesus was giving Judas the opportunity to overcome. Without the temptation, there is no proof of a real relationship with God. Falling to temptation only uncovers the unresolved issue in the heart.

This brings up an important question. Did Jesus tempt Judas? James 1:13 says: "Let no man say when he is tempted, I am tempted of God: for God cannot be tempted with evil, neither tempteth he any man." Temptation never comes from God or even from the object or person which is desired. Temptation comes from our very own flesh. You might have heard someone say, "God made me this way," speaking of a sinful nature in which the Bible clearly condemns. Such statements come from our tendency to attribute our feelings to God, However, most of the time our feelings have nothing to do with God. If we go through life following our feelings, we will live far outside the will of God. The Bible teaches we have a sinful nature, and there is a constant battle between our flesh and spirit. Paul wrote in Romans 7:18, "For I know that in me (that is, in my flesh) dwelleth no good thing," and in Romans 8:7, "the carnal mind is enmity against God: for it is not subject to the law of God, neither indeed can be."

There is no justification for saying God gave us a disposition or problem that is contrary to His very own Word.

These contradictions are the identity of the sinful flesh, not the will of God. The Bible teaches we are born with a sinful nature, and we must be born again. The thought exists—if it feels good, do it. This thought places feelings in control of how we live our lives. Because of this, people have the tendency to justify lifestyles based solely on feelings. Think about it this way: If an action is justified because of feelings, then no action is wrong. If that is true, then child molesters, murderers, rapists, liars, cheaters, and pornographers are simply misunderstood. This may seem extreme, but they are simply acting upon their feelings.

There is another tendency to justify sin as long as no one is being harmed. With this logic comes the idea of big sins and little sins. There are some who think this is the real standard for determining right and wrong. This is a very dangerous trap. It places man in the seat of God for choosing the course for one's own life. The question has to be asked: Is the Creator or the created in charge of determining what is good and what is evil?

The reality is, mankind is in the midst of a struggle between natural feelings and the nature of God. In fact, it is more than just a struggle; it is war. For people to understand who they really are, they must accept the fact there is a part of their very own nature which is in some way contrary to the nature of God. Sinful tendency is something everyone deals with. There is only one way to truly understand if something is sinful. If it is contrary to the nature of God, it is sin.

It was imperative for Judas to be faced with the choice of whether or not to commit sin. God already knows of the sin that is hidden in the heart. We must know for ourselves there is nothing we will place ahead of God. Because of this, it was necessary for Jesus to put the money bag into the hands of Judas.

God is very serious about whether we are willing to place anything ahead of Him in our lives. In Genesis 22, Abraham was asked by God to take his son up onto a mountain to sacrifice him to the Lord. God didn't really want Abraham to kill his son, but he wanted to know that Abraham would be obedient regardless of what it would cost him. Abraham had been tested many times before and had failed many of those tests. By this time in his life, he had many regrets with which to live. He had learned the hard way that disobedience brings terrible results, but obedience produces blessings. There is probably no greater sacrifice a person could give than the child of their old age. Without doubting, he took his son to obey the command. Because of his obedience, God provided another sacrifice and spared his son. Abraham's act of obedience proved his faith and set in motion a series of blessings to follow. He became known as the father of the faithful. There are many tests for those who have a high calling. As stated earlier, until we are tested, we are not beneficial to the Kingdom.

Now that we have clearly defined temptation and sin, let's take a closer look at the two possible outcomes of facing temptation. Keep in mind that being tempted is not a sin. In fact, Jesus himself was tempted in all ways like we are but never sinned. So what happens when we are tempted?

Becoming Overcomers

The first possible outcome of facing temptation is we can grow from the struggle. James 1:2-4 says, "My brethren, count it all joy when ye fall into divers temptations; knowing this, that the trying of your faith worketh patience. But let patience have her perfect work, that ye may be perfect and entire, wanting nothing."

God isn't sitting in heaven with a bucket full of lightning bolts ready to pin us down every time we slip. Instead, God, in His patience, is doing a work in our lives. As hard as it is for us to understand, we grow stronger in the Lord every time we overcome. Knowing this, we can view temptation as an opportunity instead of a hurdle. The outcome in this case is fruit being produced in our lives.

In the story of Shadrach, Meshach, and Abednego, when given the command by the wicked king to bow to the idolatrous image or be thrown into a fiery furnace, they refused to bow. They were living proof that temptation is a gauge that reveals the level of one's relationship with God. Most people would have felt that God would have to make an exception under those circumstances, but they made no excuse. God chose to miraculously keep them from any harm. Not only were they protected from the fire, but even the smell of smoke didn't get on their garments. Through the whole experience, God showed himself to be both real and all powerful. As a result of their refusing to bow, they were greatly promoted in the kingdom in which they lived.

It is important to remember they made this decision not knowing whether God would deliver them from this great threat to their comfort and their lives. This was the ultimate test. Satan presented them with the option of committing sin or being burned alive. When the writer of Hebrews spoke of all of the heroes of faith in Hebrews 11, he reminded us how many faced death faithfully, not receiving deliverance. God chose each of these people to give their lives honoring Him here on earth. In exchange, all who give their lives honoring God will be rewarded greatly throughout eternity.

One truth which is revealed in the story of Shadrach, Meshach, and Abednego is God will never allow us to face trials alone when we walk according to His Word. When the three Hebrew men were thrown into the fire, there appeared a fourth person with them. The truth is, the fourth person was already with them. Everyone else just needed to see it. God chose these three for advancement, because He knew they would remain faithful, thus glorifying Him.

I witnessed a Christian who faced a similar test in recent years. A popular reality series, which narrows down a group of contenders to a single victor, recently produced an episode where the contenders were to bow at the altar of a false god. It was known that an outspoken Christian was among the group of contenders. Giving up the opportunity to remain a contestant and receive a sizable prize, the Christian contestant refused. When asked why she didn't just pretend, she replied that it would be like sleeping with another man and telling her husband that she was thinking of him. Changing the way we think about sin doesn't change the fact that it is still sin.

Everyone is given the opportunity to overcome. No one is ordained to destruction. First Corinthians 10:13 says, "There hath no temptation taken you but such as is common to man: but God is faithful, who will not suffer you to be tempted above that which ye are able; but will with the temptation also make a way of escape, that ye may be able to bear it."

Therefore, when we fall to temptation, we have no right to blame God. He never causes us to fail. When we sin, it is because we surrender to temptation. Jesus stood by Judas until it was evident that he would never willfully let go of the love of money. Jesus didn't overcome Judas; Judas overcame Judas. David also battled temptation, and yet God said he was a man after His own heart. The difference is simple. Some people wallow in their mistakes when they fall, and some people learn from them, and get up out of the sin. Somehow all the miracles, promises, and teachings of Jesus didn't convince Judas to come clean. He chose his own destruction.

This leads us to the other outcome of sin—death. When sin is finished, it brings forth death. After Judas complained of the costly ointment being poured upon Jesus by the woman, Jesus told the disciples to leave her alone. Her motive was selfless and pure. This was the straw that broke the camel's back. Judas followed Jesus for three years. Even though Judas had been battling this temptation for some time, Satan knew this was the point where he could convince Judas to commit the ultimate act of betrayal. The Bible says Satan put it into the heart of Judas to betray Jesus. Satan had been behind this temptation the whole time. Now was his payday. Judas went to those who were looking for an opportunity to take Jesus. At least Judas was going to get something out of the deal, or so he thought. He betrayed Jesus for only thirty pieces of silver. It wouldn't have mattered if it had been all the money in the world; this was the conclusion of Satan's long battle to destroy Judas. Just like we feel when we fall to temptation, Judas immediately regretted his decision. Feeling completely overcome by sin, he took his own life without reuniting with Jesus.

The story of Judas ended with absolute devastation. He gave in fully; thus, he was defeated by Satan. However, the real story of Judas will never end. Judas didn't just disappear; no one does. There is a real man in hell today named Judas Iscariot. He is just as real as I am. Though this is difficult to ponder, he has been facing the penalty of sin for two thousand years and hasn't scratched the surface of eternity. The reality of hell should by itself be enough to convince us to turn away from sin, but people go every day losing all hope of ever escaping the consequences of their sin.

The whole process of death begins with our own lust. Judas is what the Bible calls dead, but what is the real definition of *death*? Normally, when we think of death, we think of dead bodies. James said that the body without the spirit is dead, but that statement is made only from the carnal perspective. The Bible gives numerous examples of individuals who have died physically, but have continued to exist spiritually; and many examples of individuals who have died spiritually, but have continued to exist physically. In fact, death, as God defines it, has nothing to do with our body, but only our spirit. Jesus said in John 8:52, "If a man keep my saying, he shall never see death." In John 11:25-26 He teaches: "I am the resurrection and the life: he that believeth in me, though he were dead, yet shall he live: And whosoever liveth and believeth in me shall never die."

Spiritual Death

We know everyone dies physically, but not everyone dies spiritually. Let's look back at the first promise of death in the Bible. God told Adam on the day he sinned, he would die. We know according to Scripture Adam lived physically several hundred years after he first sinned, so to what kind of death was God referring? The thing that changed for Adam was God's presence. Hence, we see that death occurs spiritually when a person is separated from God.

How does lust relate to spiritual death? Remember, sin, when it is finished, brings forth death. Sin takes place when we obey our lusts. Because sin is the thing which separates us from God, sin causes us to be spiritually dead. Sin kills! Judas was dead long before he hanged himself. His physical death was the open manifestation of what was already true spiritually. After man dies physically in sin, he is eternally exiled from the presence of God. What a warning! This is what happens when sin is finished. After someone is eternally separated from God, there is nothing else sin can do. This is the ultimate devastation for any person. Sin is then finished.

On the opposite note, after Cain killed Abel, God testified that the blood of Abel was crying out to God from the earth, giving us the first example of life after death. True death is spiritual not physical.

We opened the book by saying that Satan is singing a lullaby. The Bible calls Satan the God of this world. Second Corinthians 4:4 warns us: "The god of this world hath blinded the minds of them which believe not." Notice he didn't blind the eyes, but he blinded the minds. Satan is a mastermind at lulling minds into slumber. Satan invented sin, and he knows how to convince others to follow in his steps.

Matthew 16 tells of the time that Peter made the great confession that Jesus is the Christ. Jesus said this truth was given to Peter as a divine revelation. However, right after this, Jesus began to speak of His own suffering and death He would face. Still lacking spiritual understanding, Peter began to deny these things would happen. The rebuke from Jesus was unlike any other in Scripture. Jesus looked at Peter and said, "Get thee behind me, Satan: thou art an offence unto me: for thou savourest not the things that be of God, but those that be of men" (Matthew 16:23).

All false doctrine and sin is of Satan. In fact, 1 John 3:8 says, "He that committeth sin is of the devil." This passage speaks of the inseparable relationship between sin and Satan. We sometimes think there are big sins and small sins, and the small sins will be overlooked. We must remember the same mind that conceived the small sins also conceived the big ones. All sin is punishable by death. Whether we pay or if we allow the Atonement found in Christ's sacrificial death to pay, the punishment for sin is still death. Sin kills! This is why it is our reasonable service to live holy. We were redeemed by the precious blood of Jesus. In 2 Peter 1:3, 4 we are told, "His divine power hath given unto us all things that pertain unto life and godliness . . . that by these ye might be partakers of the divine nature, having escaped the corruption that is in the world through lust."

Jesus has equipped us with the right tools to overcome sin. The passage just mentioned speaks of escaping the corruption that is in the world, and even obtaining a divine nature. When we pursue God, our desires begin to line up with the will and nature of God. This is not something we can do for ourselves, but it is a supernatural work of grace. When we pray, fast, consume the Word of God, and commit fully unto God, we begin to go through the transformation process which takes place in the mind. It is with a renewed mind that we are able to overcome Satan's lullaby.

Questions for Thought

1. What is sin?

2. Complete the following statement: "when lust hath conceived, it bringeth forth _____"

3. Is death, as God defines it, spiritual or physical?

4. How reliable are our feelings as a determination of whether something is right or wrong?

5. Where does temptation come from?

6. What does the redemptive work of Christ give us the power to do?

Looking Back:
- Define *sin* and *death*.
- Know the source of temptation.
- Know why all people must face temptation.

Looking Forward
We will learn and explore the key fundamental building blocks which lead to complete victory of sin and Satan in the upcoming chapters. In the next chapter, we will discover the greatest tool available to believers.

SATAN'S *Lullaby*

PART THREE

Spiritual Growth

CHAPTER 6

INSPIRATION

All the commandments which I command thee this day shall ye observe to do, that ye may live, multiply, and go in and possess the land which the Lord sware unto your fathers. And thou shalt remember all the way which the Lord thy God led thee these forty years in the wilderness, to humble thee, and to prove thee, to know what was in thine heart, whether thou wouldest keep his commandments, or no. And he humbled thee, and suffered thee to hunger, and fed thee with manna, which thou knewest not, neither did thy fathers know; that he might make thee know that man doth not live by bread only, but by every word that proceedeth out of the mouth of the Lord doth man live (Deuteronomy 8:1-3).

In 2 Timothy, Paul said, "All scripture is given by inspiration of God" (3:16). The literal translation states, "All scripture is divinely breathed." Even though God used people to physically pen the words of the Bible, He is the author. The very next part of this verse says, "and is profitable for doctrine, for reproof, for correction, for instruction in righteousness" (v. 16). The Word of God is the ultimate authority that governs all things. It even determines the course of all things to come. Therefore, it is vital that all Christians learn it!

Psalm 1 happens to be my favorite passage in the entire Bible. In it, David speaks of those who meditate on God's Word day and night. He says they are like a tree planted by rivers of water. He paints a picture of a tree that brings forth fruit even in the midst of a drought. Because of its vicinity to its life source, it can't help but prosper. In contrast, he describes the wicked as the chaff that the wind blows away. Chaff is the portion of a plant that has been completely up-rooted and no longer has a life source. That is the difference between those who do and do not live their lives in total dependence on the Word of God.

Journeying With the Promises of God

I once saw a satellite photo of Egypt that illustrated this concept. From the photo, it is evident that most of Egypt is dry desert land. Few plants survive in that environment, but right down the center of Egypt runs the Nile River. For miles and miles around the river, plush green vegetation dominates the landscape. The contrast is unmistakable. It becomes apparent that the Nile overflows its banks often. It is the primary source of water for a region that is heavily populated by people, plants, and animals. When we think about the Word of God, this is the picture that God wants us to see. He wants us to know that the source of life is found only in His Word, and without His Word, there is no life.

In our key passage, Deuteronomy 8, Moses spoke to the Israelites who had survived the forty years of wilderness wandering. In verse one, he tells the Israelites if they obey the commandments, then they will live, multiply, and receive the promises of God. Verse two continues to explain the importance of their past temptations. God allowed these things so that He could prove them and know what was in their hearts. When we look at the history of the wilderness wandering, we find that God led the people of Israel through a place which had no natural resources. When we think of following God, this is not what we envision. It seemed like God was leading them into destruction. God had promised them a land flowing with milk and honey, so what did God have in mind with the wilderness? The answer is simple—it was all about trust.

At the conclusion of the wandering, the people who survived had one thing in common—they were still alive because they believed the promises of God. Death had been very selective. All who doubted and disobeyed died; all who believed and obeyed lived to receive the promise. Age was not a factor in death's selective process. Even Moses, at the age of 120, still had perfect health and eyesight when he died. The people of God learned an important lesson in the wilderness—survival didn't depend on natural resources; it depended on trusting the Word of God. They drank water from a rock; they ate bread from heaven. God was to them a cloud by day from the desert sun and a fire by night from the frigid desert cold. Their clothes and shoes never wore out. God laid out a course which ensured that only those who trusted Him would receive the promise. God did exactly what He said He would do, yet many fell short in unbelief.

The people of Israel became a tangible picture of God's spiritual principles. They taught us the natural things of the world have no effect upon the promises of God. This message was displayed from the time Moses saw the burning bush in Mount Horeb until the last parcel of ground was captured by the Israelites under the conquest of Joshua. The land of Canaan represents the eternal rest God has promised unto all who believe on His name. The land of Egypt represents the bondage in which man is under before salvation. The wilderness wandering represents the walk of faith a believer experiences in this world. These journeys represent the walk of all believers, and the dependency believers have on God's Word. There are three very important requirements which must be met for the Word of God to benefit us. In this chapter, we will highlight all three.

1. Knowing the Word

"My people are destroyed for a lack of knowledge" (Hosea 4:6). Life itself depends on the Word of God. We wouldn't be here if God had not one day said, "Let there be . . ." Life comes from God; destruction comes from Satan. The Word of God is both our origin and our defense. In Ephesians 6:17, the Word of God is called, "the sword of the Spirit." We simply cannot ward off the attacks of the Enemy when we neglect the greatest weapon provided by God. Psalm 119:11 states, "Thy word have I hid in mine heart, that I might not sin against thee."

When Jesus was tempted by the devil, three times he quoted Scripture by beginning, "It is written." Jesus didn't make an awesome display of His position in the Godhead; instead He proved that as a man, he could defeat Satan using only the Word of God.

In the United States, we have a judicial system that interprets the constitution. In theory at least, no one has been granted to sit on the absolute seat of power. All citizens are subject to words written on paper. When we violate written law, we face the condemnation of the law. It serves to protect the citizens of the United States. However, many citizens have their rights violated and don't know how to defend themselves because they don't know the law.

There is a law which has higher authority than all other law. This law has absolute power over everyone, including Satan and his kingdom. It is the written Word of God. We wouldn't expect an unlearned attorney to protect us in court, so why do we think that spiritual ignorance is any better? As Christians, we will never be able to receive our God-given rights if we don't know what they are. Even Jesus said in John 12, He wouldn't judge the unbeliever, but the unbeliever would be judged by the words that he had already spoken.

Until we as Christians put away the distractions, pick up the Word of God, and put it in our hearts, there is no way that we will ever become spiritually strong enough to fully withstand the attacks of Satan. The easiest way that Satan can destroy a person is to keep them from the Word of God. In the parable of the sower and the seed, Satan is pictured as a bird that steals away the seed a farmer is intending to plant. He doesn't crave the seed, but is afraid of it reproducing. The seed is the Word of God. Satan knows when a person is endued with the Word of God, he is a serious threat to his kingdom. So where do we start?

No one is born a giant. There must be a growth period. First Peter 2:2 says, "As newborn babes, desire the sincere milk of the word, that ye may grow thereby." Most Christians at some point become discouraged about what they don't know. We should continue to strive and rejoice in continual growth. Even the apostle Paul said he had not yet "attained." We will never reach a point where we are finished until we reach Heaven. There is always room for growth.

In the parable of the sower and the seed, the only ground that brought forth produce had been prepared to receive the seed. Being prepared takes planning. We must set aside time to study His Word. When we do, we should remove the distractions, open up ourselves, and invite God to plant into our lives whatever portion of seed He chooses. He is the farmer; we are the field. When we prepare ourselves, and then receive the Word into our hearts, it is like seed planted in fertile ground—fruit will be produced.

The tendency of most believers is to allow others to spoon-feed them all they will ever know about the Word of God. Try something. Take a black and white page of a book. Make a copy of it. Take that copy and make another copy. Continue that process of making more copies of copies and notice what begins to happen. Even if the highest quality copiers are used, eventually the page will become unreadable. The same principle applies to those who only know about the Scriptures through other people. Most people seldom read the Bible and take the Scripture at face value; instead they tend to first believe what they have always heard others say. When we stand before the throne of God, we will be judged according to the Word of God, not the word of our preacher, parents, or mentors.

We sometimes forget the sacrifice that many have paid to pass down the Word of God from generation to generation. What a disservice it would be to shelve the wonderful gift that has been passed down to us. How privileged we are to be able to own and study the pages of Scripture. May we never forget it.

2. Believing the Word

"The word . . . did not profit them, not being mixed with faith in them that heard it" (Hebrews 4:2). A few years back, while having some dental work done, the dentist used a technique I had never seen. He used a type of filling that, when exposed to a flash of light, hardened immediately. Instead of having to wait, he flashed the light and said "all done." I asked how the filling hardened so quickly. He explained that the light was a catalyst which activated the hardening pro-cess. Instantly, the filling was cured. The Word of God has an activator as well. It is called faith. Without faith, the Word of God cannot benefit us. Hebrews 11:6 says, "Without faith it is impossible to please him: for he that cometh to God must believe that he is, and that he is a rewarder of them that dil-igently seek him."

Faith brings total transformation to our lives. In fact, faith gives us the ability to allow the promises of God to change our course of action without any doubt His promises will come to pass. Faith causes us to believe God and not our own perspective. A Christian must walk by faith, not by sight. When we have faith, we accept that God knows better than we do.

Abraham, known as the "father of Israel," was called by God to journey from his home at the very seat of civilization to another land—what would become known as the Prom-ised Land. So, "he went out, not knowing whither he went" (Hebrews 11:8). The Bible attributes this to faith. The sim-ple obedience of Abraham required that he trust God with his own life. Would we take such a step? For someone to receive God's promises, God requires the believer to initi-ate the promise with a step of faith. God doesn't just drop the promise into our laps, but requires we take action before there is any physical proof the promise will come to pass. God expects us to trust Him. Proverbs 3:5 tells us to, "Trust in the Lord with all thine heart; and lean not unto thine own understanding."

Keep in mind that we can claim only what God has truly promised. If God promised it, then it is ours for the claim-ing. If you have ever lost luggage at an airport, then you know what I mean. When you go to baggage claims, you must show your claim ticket or ID. We can't just take what we like; we get what has our name on it. Some think that faith is the ability to get whatever is desired. That is not how faith works. Many failures can be attributed to man thinking on God's behalf. He doesn't need any help. His plan for our lives was completed before we were ever born. We can, however, claim that which God has promised us. No one can take that away.

Faith activates the promises of God, but doubt voids them. When Jesus went to His hometown, the Bible says that He was astonished at their lack of faith. Because of this, many great works were withheld. The key to unlocking the promises of God is believing that He will fulfill them, even when the worldly odds are stacked against them. God is not a gambler; He is an ensurer. Jesus told a centurion in Matthew 8:13, "As thou hast believed, so be it. . . unto thee."

God has sent forth His Word, but it is up to us to receive His promises by faith. Let's look at a promise of God that guarantees victory over Satan. Luke 10:19 says, "Behold, I give you power to tread on serpents and scorpions, and over all the power of the enemy: and nothing shall by any means hurt you."

This passage speaks of the authority a true believer has over demonic forces. What a wonderful promise, yet many will never benefit from it because of fear. Fear is a byproduct of doubt. It is the opposite of faith, and may be the biggest reason people miss out on God's promises. I am often encouraged by the stories in Scripture which show the journey from fear to faith. I love reading about how God delivered Israel from oppression through the unlikely, untrained hand of Gideon. There were many fears he had to overcome in order to become the man that God called him to be. Moses and Jeremiah also had notable "I can't" moments, but learned otherwise. God has big things in store for us as well. Can we believe it?

3. Obeying the Word

> Faith, if it hath not works, is dead, being alone.
> Yea, a man may say, Thou hast faith, and I have
> works: shew me thy faith without thy works, and
> I will shew thee my faith by my works. Thou
> believest that there is one God; thou doest well:
> the devils also believe, and tremble. But wilt thou
> know, O vain man, that faith without works is
> dead? (James 2:17-20).

Obedience is the condition God places upon His promises. So often, we void the promises of God in our lives through disobedience. It is important to understand that faith alone isn't enough in our Christian walk.

How can people show their belief without corresponding actions? It is impossible. Faith without works is dead. The Bible doesn't say the just shall *have* faith; it says the just shall *live by* their faith. How can we say we have faith if we require God to first show tangible proof of His promises before we step out? What if Noah waited to see rain before he built the ark? What if we wait until we think we can afford it before we commit to tithe? Faith requires us to put our security on the line. God wants us to know that we can depend on His promises more than our resources.

One of the greatest examples of the cost of disobedience in the Bible is the death of Moses without being able to enter the Promised Land. In Numbers 20, we find the story of the Israelites in the desert of Zin. Because there was no water, the people murmured against Moses. The Lord told Moses to speak to the rock commanding water to come forth. Instead, Moses struck the rock as he had done once before. It took only one verse with no second chance for God to inform Moses he was no longer a recipient of the Promised Land.

The Book of Hebrews brings strong examples from the wilderness wandering to give us a New Testament carryover of the same concept. Hebrew 4:1 says, "Let us therefore fear, lest, a promise being left us of entering into his rest, any of you should seem to come short of it."

The Bible lists numerous examples of people who have squandered the promises of God through disobedience. We read of Adam, Saul, Eli, Achan, Judas, Lucifer; the list goes on and on. Sometimes the list consisted of whole nations at a time, including on occasion, the nation of Israel. This should serve as a warning to us. We must understand and fulfill the conditions God places upon His blessings. Oftentimes, people apply the principle of God's love to His promises. That cannot be done. God's love is unconditional, but His promises are not. Ephesians 5:5-6 says:

> For this ye know, that no whoremonger, nor unclean person, nor covetous man, who is an idolater, hath any inheritance in the kingdom of Christ and of God. Let no man deceive you with vain words: for because of these things cometh the wrath of God upon the children of disobedience.

These sins are all examples of disobedience. This scripture bears out that those who do these things have no Godly inheritance. The warning is strong; "Let no man deceive you." Disobedience brings the wrath of God.

Paul made it clear in Romans 2 that not the *hearers* of the Word are justified, but the *doers* of the Word are justified. When applying this truth to Scriptures like the Sermon on the Mount, we are faced with areas of obedience that take the Christian experience to a whole new level. After hearing Jesus make a statement such as "Love your enemy," we have to act in a way that requires supernatural strength. The mandates of the kingdom of God push us to a level of commitment that takes full surrender. This is what faith is all about.

We have the tendency to think it is ok to "water down" the obedience issue. However, we have to realize a change in us must first come before we are ready to receive God's promises. It is futile to attempt to obtain the promises of God without any real change in our lives. Change is not comfortable, but it is incredibly necessary. Obedience makes a definite change in our lives. As we move farther into obedience, we become more like Christ in our character. Love and forgiveness are among the hardest areas of obedience for us, but these are probably the most likely to impart a noticeable change in us. Scripture plainly states if we don't forgive, we can't be forgiven. What an eye-opening thought. This is a clear example of the direct correlation between obedience to God and receiving His promises.

It goes without saying that this whole process can be an incredible challenge. That is really the whole point. God is challenging us and moving us toward transformation. This involves a clearing out of the old ways in our lives to make room for the new. His Word is the key to understanding how to allow God to accomplish His perfect work in us. We must *know* it, *believe* it, and *obey* it. When we do, then Satan has no power over us. As we learned in Deuteronomy 8, if we do these things, we will live, multiply, and receive the promises of God.

Questions for Thought:

1. Who inspired all the scriptures of the Bible?

2. What is the ultimate authority that governs all things?

3. What are the three requirements that must be met in order for the Word of God to benefit someone?

4. In the parable of the sower and the seed, what was different about the ground that yielded a crop?

5. What activates the promises of God?

6. What condition does God place on all His promises?

Looking Back:
- All Scripture is inspired by God.
- Understand the Word of God is the foundation for all truth, life, and hope.
- To receive the promises of God, one must know, believe, and obey His Word.

Looking Forward:
In the discovery of truth, life, and hope, there is more than meets the eye for a believer who truly seeks God's way. Chapter 7 will delve into that topic.

REVELATION

"Blessed are the pure in heart: for they shall see God"
(Matthew 5:8).

So far in this book, the main topic has been the fundamentals of living above sin. That is important, but there is much more to the Christian experience than mere survival in a world of satanic influence. As we saw in the previous chapter, the Word of God is the key to living victoriously. However, this is only the beginning of an amazing journey. If these fundamentals are followed on the surface only, we miss the very thing God wants us to discover most of all—*Him*. In a discussion with the disciples about the meaning of His parables, Jesus explained there are those who seeing, didn't perceive, and hearing, didn't understand. Jesus continued by saying not all people would be given understanding. There is an incredible discovery reserved only for those who are not satisfied with the status quo in their relationship with God. When searching the Scriptures, things such as doctrine, principle, and promise are evident. However, revelation belongs only to those who truly put God at the very center of all they do.

To lay the foundation for this topic, let's take a look at the meaning of the word *revelation*. There are things that

God puts in front of us which are impossible to miss. There are other things that are hidden. The things that are hidden can only be realized when God makes them known. The root of the word *revelation* is "reveal." When God shows us the hidden things, this is what we call revelation. It should be noted that revelation never supersedes truth. The fundamental doctrines of truth are plainly spelled out in Scripture and are for everyone to know and understand. It is false doctrine to believe that any person has special rights to the information contained therein. Even when someone is permitted to prophesy in the church, the Bible tells us that there should be others standing by to judge or discern the integrity of the word given. God's words always come with divine confirmation. When people claim divine revelation to make themselves more important, it is certainly not of God. A true sign of genuine revelation is the glorification of God.

Most revelation is personal and only gives a deeper understanding of what we already know. It may be inexplicable to others. For instance, we can try to explain that Grandma's seven-layer chocolate cake is good, but until it is tasted, the truth about it can never be fully known. The Scriptures tell us to taste and see that the Lord is good. Only when we taste, do we realize the magnitude of truth.

The Reason for Revelation

There is a reason that God designed revelation this way. You might have noticed that some people never seem to see God in anything. Revelation has no value to them. Those who are seekers may find God in any number of ways. He can be found in answered prayers or needs miraculously met. God has no limits in revealing Himself. He can be found in the grocery store or in a sunrise.

Once, I knew for sure God had lain on my heart to place the only $10 I had in my wallet in an offering plate. I knew this was my gas money to get home. Before the age of debit cards, this presented a real problem . . . but not for God. It became very clear to me this was what God was asking me to do; so, I obeyed. After church, someone who knew nothing about the need placed a $100 bill in my hand. I had not told anyone what I had done, nor had I asked for anything. God was revealing Himself in my life. That simple act of obedience turned out to be the first in a chain reaction of events which brought my family into the ministry. I have had many such experiences. These experiences have firmly etched the certainty of God's existence in my mind.

However, God will only reveal Himself on His own terms. Many people allow God into their lives, but only on their terms. We are fortunate that He allows us into fellowship with Him at all. It is incredibly arrogant to give God conditions to our relationship with Him. But because of this, some people will never see God or fully understand His love for us.

The Importance of Revelation

Why is revelation so important? Proverbs 29:18 says, "Where there is no vision, the people perish." The *New International Version* gives a slightly more nuanced interpretation. It says, "Where there is no revelation, people cast off restraint."

When God doesn't speak to people, they are on a downhill slope toward destruction. There are a few times in the Old Testament which record there was no open vision in that day, but every man did what was right in his own eyes. In other words, God wasn't on speaking terms with His people, and man's imagination ran wild. The reason God allowed that degree of separation is plainly explained in the Bible. Romans 1:21 says, "When they knew God, they glorified him not as God, neither were thankful."

God must be approached with reverence and passion. The only way to experience His presence is to glorify Him. After the fall of man, the Bible tells us that God still showed up to tangibly encounter man for a short period of time. A few generations later, the Bible says, "Then began men to call upon the name of the Lord" (Genesis 4:26). Since that time, it has been understood that an encounter with God is a true privilege. When we don't see it that way, we won't see Him. God has still made Himself available, but only to those who will seek Him on His terms. Acts 17:27-28 says God made mankind to "seek the Lord, if haply they might feel after him, and find him, though he be not far from every one of us: For in him we live, and move, and have our being."

We were created to search. It is not God's pleasure to remain hidden from us. He wants us to discover Him. He has given us the tools to find Him. Without searching, we will miss out on the best that He has to offer. God is not withholding the greatest things, He is reserving them. Psalm 84:11 says, "No good thing will he withhold from them that walk uprightly."

The process of revelation begins with repentance and salvation. Jesus' first sermon content recorded in the Bible is, "Repent ye: for the kingdom of heaven is at hand" (Matthew 3:2). Repentance is the simple key to salvation. Without repentance we cannot know God. The word *repent* means "to turn around." When we repent, we turn from the nature of fallen man and return to the nature of created man. Jesus followed the command to repent with the Sermon on the Mount.

The Revelation of the Beatitudes

The Sermon on the Mount began with nine statements that are now known as the Beatitudes. The Beatitudes can be found in Matthew 5:3-12. Reading these principles for the godly life can leave us feeling a little turned around. This is because our nature gravitates toward the nature of fallen man. Everything we read in the Beatitudes is against human nature. Jesus never once violated any of these nine principles, and He did it with the same strength that is available to us today.

The first principle says, "Blessed are the poor in spirit: for theirs is the kingdom of heaven" (Matthew 5:3). There is a blessing, but also a qualification for the blessing. This is the same format used in all nine of the Beatitudes. To be poor in spirit means to be humble. Being humble is the foundational principle that all the rest is built upon. We cannot advance to the next principle until we have fully adopted humility as a way of life.

The key to the entire sermon is given in Matthew 5:8: "Blessed are the pure in heart: for they will see God." Nothing about this passage tells us this verse will only be fulfilled after we die. When we think of seeing someone, we picture physical characteristics. That is not what this verse is describing. Hebrews 11:27 speaks of Moses, saying: "By faith he forsook Egypt, not fearing the wrath of the king: for he endured, as seeing him who is invisible." How did Moses see God? In this verse, God was described as being invisible. If God is invisible, how is it possible for someone to see Him?

The Revelation of Holiness

Matthew 5:8 explains the requirement for anyone who will see God. It says "the pure in heart" will see God. Hebrews 12:14 corroborates this—"Follow . . . holiness, without which no man shall see the Lord."

97

Holiness is God's standard for living. Man's traditions or cultures do not have a monopoly on the definition of holiness. Only the Bible can define what it means to be holy— walking in repentance and purity. In pursuing holiness, we create an environment for God to reveal Himself to us. Oftentimes, the first revelation we experience is our unworthiness and lowliness before the Lord. A good example of this is found in Isaiah 6 when Isaiah had a vision of the Lord in the Temple. The angels cried "Holy, holy, holy," and then Isaiah cried "Woe is me" (vv. 3-5). He realized his sinfulness and repented. After repenting, God separated him from his sin. That's the process. We repent, and then God changes our nature.

When we understand that purity is the standard for revelation, we understand why Jesus said that a wicked and perverse generation seeks for a sign. They seek for a sign because even when signs are all around them, they cannot discern Him. Jesus once asked Phillip, "Have I been so long time with you, and yet hast thou not known me?" (John 14:9). This is what Jesus meant when he said, "seeing, they may see and not perceive" (Mark 4:12). It is one thing to know about the man named Jesus, it is something else to truly know Him. After Peter's assertion that Jesus was indeed the Messiah who had been long awaited and promised, Jesus told him that was a revelation from the Father. Even walking with Jesus wasn't enough to truly know Him; there had to be an element revealed to him by the Father. The same is true for us. To truly know Jesus, there must be a revelation in our lives. John 1:10 speaks of Jesus by saying, "He was in the world, and the world was made by him, and the world knew him not."

Even the biological brothers of Jesus didn't know who He was until after His resurrection. However, John the Baptist knew who He was immediately. The Bible explains that God had given Him that specific revelation. In another passage, Jesus wept over the city of Jerusalem because its inhabitants didn't realize that their king had visited them. All these examples point to revelation as being necessary. First Corinthians 2:9-12 says:

> Eye hath not seen, nor ear heard, neither have entered into the heart of man, the things which God hath prepared for them that love him. But God hath revealed them unto us by his Spirit: for the Spirit searcheth all things, yea, the deep things of God. For what man knoweth the things of a man, save (except) the spirit of man which is in him? Even so the things of God knoweth no man, but the Spirit of God. Now we have received, not the spirit of the world, but the spirit which is of God; that we might know the things that are freely given to us of God.

The Revelation of the Holy Spirit

This passage clues us in on our topic. The Spirit reveals the deep things of God. To receive revelation, we must see through the eyes of the Holy Spirit, not our own. Verse 14 tells us: "But the natural man receiveth not the things of the Spirit of God: for they are foolishness unto him: neither can he know them, because they are spiritually discerned."

This is why some people will never see God working in their lives. Most of us know people who think that what Christians believe is foolishness. We need not wonder why. They are consumed with embracing themselves instead of embracing God.

When the wise men came looking for Jesus, (the newborn king), the people of Israel sat in the shadows while foreign

Magi received the revelation of His birth. Maybe their desire to seek Him out to worship Him was the reason why. They left their kingdoms behind, brought expensive gifts, and totally interrupted their lives to experience a moment with the Messiah. Most people wouldn't cross the street for an experience with God. It might require change. In Psalm 27, David unveiled the greatest desire of his heart. He wanted only to dwell in the house of the Lord. The reason for his desire wasn't so he could live in the lap of luxury. David wanted to behold the beauty of the Lord and be able to inquire of Him. In response to David's desire, verse 8 tells us God commanded David to seek His face. David's enthusiastic reply let God know that David would pursue God with everything. David understood a very important fact—a supernatural revelation leads to supernatural living.

Fruitful in and Out of Season

In the previous chapter of this book, we discussed the Psalm 1 principle of being like a tree planted by a river. Building on what has been discussed about revelation in this chapter; we will take a look at a story found in Mark 11. In this chapter, Jesus was entering into Jerusalem one particular morning and was hungry. He saw a fig tree from a distance that had leaves. The Bible says that he supposed it had figs on it, but fig season had not yet come. When Jesus found no fruit, he cursed the tree, and it died. Why would Jesus express anger toward an inanimate object? Was he simply losing His temper, or did He have an object lesson in mind? To expect figs in season is natural. To expect them out of season is supernatural. Paul told Timothy to be prepared both in season and out of season, but how is it possible to be prepared out of season?

Several years ago, I was hired to build tables for a hydroponic greenhouse system. I had never heard this term before. In a hydroponic greenhouse, vegetables can be grown without the use of dirt. Water channels were used to feed the plants nutrients by hydration. The greenhouse temperature was carefully controlled by a water-cooling device. I didn't fully grasp the purpose of all this precise effort until I witnessed veggies being harvested in the middle of January. In fact, there was a never-ending season of harvest. Resources were not acquired randomly, they were planned intentionally. When we live according to the random seasonal resources of our natural surroundings, we are much like the fig tree of Mark 11. This is not acceptable to Jesus. He has supernatural expectations; therefore, our faith must have a supernatural supply.

In the last chapter of the Bible, John the Revelator is being shown a river described as a pure river of living water. This river flows from the throne of God. At the river is a tree known as the "Tree of Life." This tree has supernatural traits. It grows twelve kinds of fruit, and it produces year-round. The type tree is not what makes the tree supernatural. The source from which it draws its nutrients is the key. The river doesn't send random selections of seasonal nutrients. Its ingredients are precisely prepared by God himself.

God has a specially prepared supply for us as well. When we are planted by the river flowing from the throne of God, our fruitfulness never ends. In Scripture, the Holy Spirit is often described as either running water or rain. Being watered by the Holy Spirit, we produce the fruit of the Spirit. For example, the Bible talks about a peace that surpasses understanding, in other words, a peace that is so deep it is beyond comprehension. When a person has just been given a piece of information that should shake them to the core, but they retain their faith, courage, and peace, this indicates that their Source isn't random or seasonal; it is intentional.

The Process of Revelation

So how does revelation take our faith to the place of deep fulfillment? To answer this question, Philippians 4:19 says, "My God shall supply all your need according to his riches in glory by Christ Jesus." Hearing this verse should calm our fears and bring us peace, but for some it has less impact than for others. However, when life is tested, God reveals Himself to those who truly seek Him. It is by seeing evidence of God working in our lives during difficult times that we are able to grasp the reality of what the Scriptures promise. This helps us learn to turn our doubts over to God with a sincere heart of worship and know God is supremely superior to our problems. Doing this, we may begin to expect victory even before we see the physical proof of it. A revelation of God's presence changes our total outlook and experience through life. Simply put, we don't just see a promise; we see God. This is why revelation is a vital part of a Christian's life. It is through revelation that our faith becomes supernatural.

Almost everyone has heard of David's encounter with Goliath. During that experience, David proved to be the real spiritual giant. However, he wasn't born with supernatural faith. He had to face moments of difficulty to learn God was truly faithful in the most intimidating circumstances. God used him in areas we might consider unimportant to help him grow to the faith he would one day need to be king. He learned God would give him victory in the small battles first. When wild animals threatened his sheep, he learned to trust in God to deliver them. Realistically, he would have lost only a sheep or two, but God had begun to prove Himself. Once he saw God at work in little ways, he began to trust God in big ways. The Bible doesn't say how many times David had to fend off smaller animals before he had the faith to fend off lions and bears or even if his faith was strong enough to trust God for protection right away. But David learned what applied to wild animals such as lions and bears also applied to giants. He discovered God had no limitations. David's experience caused him to be aware of God's presence. Awareness of God's presence ensured him of God's promises. It was with this surety that David could stand before the giant without any fear. This was truly a supernatural moment made possible by supernatural faith. This is the result of revelation. God wants all of us to come to the same place in our faith David had come to in his. When we allow God to transform our faith with His revelation, then He can transform our entire life.

Questions for Thought:

1. What is it God wants us to discover most of all?

2. What is the meaning of the word *revelation*?

3. What is a sign of a true revelation?

4. Why is revelation so important?

5. What attitude should we have when we seek God?

6. According to Matthew 5:8, who has the privilege of revelation?

7. What is God's standard for living?

Looking Back:
- Understand the definition of *revelation*.
- Know the requirements we must meet in order to receive revelation from God.
- Be able to give the definition of holiness and know how to seek it.

Looking Forward:
In the final chapter, we will explore the changed life of the believer who has applied the principles given by God to mankind.

CHAPTER 8

TRANSFORMATION

"But we all, with open face beholding as in a glass the glory of the Lord, are changed into the same image from glory to glory, even as by the Spirit of the Lord" (2 Corinthians 3:18).

Many years ago, my wife and I began to experience a radical desire to have a deeper relationship with the Lord. We wanted to know Him like never before. We were so hungry for His presence we committed every spare moment to prayer and the study of His Word. We set aside every Thursday for complete fasting. We both knew there was a ministerial calling on our lives, but were unsure when and where it would take us. We had made steep sacrifices to remain available for the ministry. In fact, just after we were married, I was offered a job in Florida which I considered to be a once-in-a-lifetime opportunity. Without a second thought, we turned down the job, because it would have hindered the possibility of advancement into the ministry. We believed open doors were right around the corner. To our dismay, five years passed, and we were still waiting for that advancement. Discouragement began to set in. I had been called into the ministry, but I was still working at a local manufacturing facility. We had involved ourselves in jail and prison ministry, nursing home ministry, and teaching Sunday school. Those ministries were important, but we knew there was much more to our calling than what we were doing. We ended up at such a point of desperation we began praying a prayer that changed the rest of our lives.

It was during that time we really learned how to pray effectively. Before this point in our lives, we had the impression God was in a distant place where He could hear us, but we couldn't hear Him; but He showed us how wrong we were. God began to open doors which eventually led us to where we are today. All along, God was simply waiting for us to reach the point of total submission. When we determined that God could have His way no matter what, He began to do incredible things in our lives. This is the life-changing prayer we learned to pray way back then:

"Lord, change us. Make us the people You would have us to be. Do whatever it takes. Not our will, but Yours be done."

Surrendering Our Hearts

To tell the truth, we were afraid to say those words. I had the crazy thought God might bring terrible circumstances into our lives because I had given Him the invitation. Instead of an outbreak of catastrophes, an unusual peace began to settle in. Through a heart of surrender, we were already on the path to becoming the people God wanted us to be. This verbalized prayer was simply the outcome of such surrender. Our prayer life was transformed and became meaningful. As time went on, His will seemed to come into focus. We began to receive confidence to do anything the Lord asked us to do. In fact, we discovered He was much closer than we had ever known. His presence became so real to our lives that we had a new desire to tell everyone about Him. It was no longer out of responsibility; it was out of passion.

Serving Him became the number one desire of our hearts. Each new day, we experienced a new outpouring of His love. We learned that ministry was about where we were at any given time. I soon began to meet with a small number of believers every day during break time at work. We started a prayer and devotion group which met right in the center of the manufacturing plant. I became a pastor of a different sort. This "house church" grew tremendously. People whom I thought would never be reached came and listened to the Word as we took turns sharing from the Bible each day. Many lives were changed as a result of this outreach which would last for many more years. As time went on, revival began to spring up into other areas of our lives. God showed us genuine ministry couldn't be confined; it followed us everywhere we went.

Eventually, we accepted a part-time position as youth pastors at a nearby church. After being there only three months, we grew very suspicious of things going on that shouldn't have been. These were events that we knew would shake the congregation to its core. We took the advice of my closest mentor and decided to leave before the harmful impact came. We knew if our suspicions were correct, it was going to get messy. The misconduct did finally come to light, and it was worse than what we had expected. Nonetheless, it took a very long time for it to all come out. During that time of uncertainty, we lost much sleep wondering if leaving had been the right decision.

One week, back at my home church, my pastor scheduled me to preach the upcoming Wednesday night service. That Wednesday morning, however, I found myself battling inside like never before over the decision we had made to leave the youth pastor position. I didn't feel like I was in any condition to preach. I left work early that day to talk to my pastor about how I was feeling. I showed up at church with three questions that I intended to ask him. When I arrived, he looked at me and said, "I have been waiting for you." That was odd considering that I should have been at work. We walked into his office, and he opened a drawer to retrieve an envelope with that day's date on it. Many months earlier, in prayer, he was led of the Lord to write down three things to give me on that particular day. The three things written down were the answers to the three questions that I had intended to ask. God showed me in that moment I had been right in the center of His will the whole time. He also showed me why things had happened the way they did. All of this was written down before I had ever been offered the youth pastor position at the other church. I cannot explain the peace God brought to my life that day. I knew for certain that His favor was on my life.

As time went on, my wife and I moved into other opportunities of ministry. As the years have gone by, God has proven Himself time and time again in many ways. It was through the tough times that God molded us. We may still have a long way to go, but we can say with confidence God has transformed us. We learned that total surrender defines a Christian. Without total surrender, the outcome of ministry remains human-sized, not God-sized.

There is a calling on everyone's life, but no one will reach their greatest potential until he or she comes to the place of total submission. When this happens, God begins moving a believer into his or her rightful place. The Church suffers when individuals don't reach their full potential. Christ is the head, but we are the body. God expects us to do our part. In the Book of Ephesians, Paul talks about unity in the diverse body of Christ. He says that growth will continue to occur until we, as one body, measure up to the fullness of Christ's stature.

For us to fulfill our part in God's kingdom, He must lead us down a road which leads to total submission. Our willingness often determines how rocky the road will be. Unfortunately, many will never complete the journey to full surrender, but will live their lives constantly seeking for but never finding true fulfillment. People oftentimes look many places trying to find the "secret of success." However, the foundation of success in our Christian life is simple—total surrender. Without it, no real success can occur. Transformation really begins to happen when we reach a point of total submission. The first two steps in the transformation process have to do with inspiration, and revelation. *Inspiration* is "the understanding of the Word of God." *Revelation* is the "uncovering of the person of God." *Transformation* is "the change wrought in us by God as we seek His will."

The Transforming Glory of God

In Exodus, an example is given of the power of God's glory. After the people of Israel were delivered from Egyptian bondage, they began making their journey toward Sinai. This was the place where God had chosen to reveal Himself and speak with His people. God didn't choose Egypt because they had not yet taken the step of faith, nor did He choose Canaan because His promises would have already been tangibly delivered. He chose a time and place where they had to totally depend upon God's promise. When they arrived, Moses went up into the mountain.

In Exodus 19:5-6, God called Moses and told Him to tell the people of Israel these words: "If ye will obey my voice indeed, and keep my covenant, then ye shall be a peculiar treasure unto me above all people; for all the earth is mine: And ye shall be unto me a kingdom of priests, and an holy nation." God gives both promises and commandments. It is paramount that we embrace both. The only real hope available to this world comes from the words God speaks. Moses was instructed to have the people sanctify themselves. In three days, God was going to descend upon the mountain in both audible and visible form. God had given the people of Israel the command to stand at the foot of the mountain during this time. However, Exodus 20:18-21 reads:

> And all the people saw the thunderings, and the lightings, and the noise of the trumpet, and the mountain smoking: and when the people saw it, they removed, and stood afar off. And they said unto Moses, Speak thou with us, and we will hear: but let not God speak with us, lest we die. And Moses said unto the people, Fear not: for God is come to prove you, and that his fear may be before your faces, that ye sin not. And the people stood afar off, and Moses drew near unto the thick darkness where God was.

This was a sad moment for the people of Israel. God desired them to draw close, but instead, they stood far off. Sadly, that is the same perspective most believers have of God—they stand far off. This is not God's will for any of us. He desires to fill us with His glory, but for that to happen, we must first draw close.

The events of that day set in motion a division in the people of Israel. Moses and another select few continually drew closer to God, but everyone else drifted farther away. While Moses was transformed into the glorious image of the One with whom he spent time, the people of Israel conformed to the world and its practices. The people of that generation subsequently fell dead in the wilderness never receiving the best of what God had to offer.

Having been in God's presence, something unique happened to Moses. His experience left him hungry for even more. Moses petitioned God to show him the fullness of His glory. God honored that request. Even though God didn't allow Moses to see His face, he did allow Moses to witness Him pass by in His glory. This became the greatest moment of his life. There are no words to express what Moses experienced that day.

When we catch a glimpse of God in His strength and majesty, we recognize that nothing can stand against His will. This keeps both fear and rebellion at bay. We were made for God's presence. Once in His presence, we become charged with the essence of life that created us. Only then do we realize our true potential. When we, the creation, come into the presence of the Creator, the reality of our sinful state is exposed in the light of His purity and holiness. Without that experience, we cannot gain the identity God intends for us to have. Subsequently, we cannot reveal God to the world around us. There is a true connection between grasping His glorious nature and understanding the expression of true life.

At the point that we are brought face to face with the glory of God, His glory begins to reproduce itself in us. This is how the transformation process begins, and this is exactly what happened to Moses. As he descended from the mountain, he didn't know His face glowed with the glory of God. He reflected the image of the One with whom he had spent time. This transformation process is described in 2 Corinthians 3:18: "We all, with open face beholding as in a glass the glory of the Lord, are changed into the same image."

Second Corinthians 3, talks about the transforming glory of God. In this chapter, Paul compared the New Testament glory with the Old Testament glory. Moses represented the Old Testament glory which was temporary. After the mountaintop experience, his face shone so much the people of Israel were afraid to look at him. In order to instruct the people, Moses had to wear a veil while in their presence. They refused to witness the glory of the Lord.

It is true the presence of God's glory can make us uncomfortable. This is because at first, our nature has so much changing to do. Feelings of guilt and shame are natural. At the same time, His grace is overwhelming. It becomes the perfect environment for surrender. We realize the appeal of His presence, and want more of it. However, something in our nature fights our desire to surrender. We must let go! There should be a letting go of our corrupt nature and a holding on to His glorious person. When we allow our corrupt nature to dominate our choice to draw close or stand off, we will find ourselves like the Israelites in this story. Because of their refusal, they would never go through the transformation process, and they would not receive the promise.

Second Corinthians 3:18 describes the New Testament glory which is eternal. This passage reveals one of the greatest truths in Scripture. When we, the New Testament church, come into the presence of God, we behold His glory with an open face. This means that He is not wearing a veil. The passage states that His image becomes as clear as looking into a mirror. When this happens, the natural glory of our person becomes transformed into the image of the glory of God. The New Testament glory available to us is much greater than the glory Moses experienced. In fact, just as the sun overpowers the stars in the daytime, the Old Testament glory is overshadowed by the New Testament glory which is reflected in us.

TRANSFORMATION

Spending Time in His Presence

There is no doubt the Church today is lacking good examples of this principle. So, why aren't Christians everywhere bearing the image of Christ? I heard the result of a Christian survey on the radio. I was shocked to find out the average self-proclaimed Christian prays less than one minute a day! No wonder most believers aren't Christlike. For the transformation process to take place, we must spend time in His presence.

So where do we begin? First, we must read His Word on a daily basis. In the wilderness wandering, the provision of manna was a picture of Christians consuming the Word of God. The people were only allowed to gather enough manna for that day's use. They were expected to gather fresh manna daily. God provides our "daily bread," and today's manna won't suffice for tomorrow. The Word of God is our nourishment, so we may learn to depend on His provision and grow strong in His image.

As Christians, we long for God's power in our lives. However, if we don't walk like Jesus, talk like Jesus, see as Jesus sees, hear like Jesus hears, and become altogether like Jesus, then how can we expect to receive the supernatural things of Jesus? The Word of God is spiritual seed, and the same seed that produces fruit in our lives also produces power. Life has many tests so that we can know where we really stand in Him. Jesus once pointed out that the tree is known by its fruit. If the fruit of the Spirit isn't the leading force in all our responses to life, then we know the seed hasn't completed its work. We must keep planting. Supernatural transformation takes place only on the firm foundation of the Word of God.

Spending Time in Prayer

We must also cultivate our lives through prayer. For a young Christian, learning how to pray can be a challenge. In the process of learning, we should learn to pray for God's will to be accomplished in us. I personally learned how to pray using an open Bible. I found His Word can easily direct our prayers toward effectiveness. Prayer should be a continual activity for Christians. In fact, Jesus, being the Son of God, made Himself our example by remaining in constant communication with the Father. If Jesus needed to pray, without any doubt, we need to pray. Jesus prayed often, sometimes spending all night in prayer. He also allocated certain locations specifically for prayer. Following His example, we must form the habit of praying regularly. We must not allow Satan to make us think our prayers aren't effective. God accepts the prayers of a repentant person. His ears are open to the righteous. When we combine reading God's Word with prayer, God reveals to us the meaning of Scripture and the purpose of our lives.

The Need for Fasting

In addition to consuming the Word and cultivating our lives in prayer, we must also fast. This might be a brand new concept to many believers, but it is very important. It is during times of fasting that we capture the heart of God. According to Isaiah, fasting is what causes us to have the desire to deal our bread to the hungry, bring the poor into our homes, and clothe the naked. We mentioned in the last chapter that the beatitudes can leave us feeling turned around. This is because our human nature is opposite of God's nature. Our nature is selfish; but God's nature is selfless. Fasting is one of the most effective ways to change our innermost being so that we may be able to reflect God's nature. Our reward becomes the glory of the Lord.

Many Christians today do not realize the need for fasting. I have discovered those who don't fast have a belief that it is too extreme or overzealous. I have also found those who don't see the importance of fasting stare at me with disbelief when I speak of some of the miracles that I have witnessed. God's revelation is very selective. Fasting with a genuine desire to experience His presence yields amazing results.

Almost all the advancements in ministry, the miracles, and the incredible experiences which have proven God's presence in my life have happened during times of fasting. Fasting started the ball rolling for me in ministry. This pattern also applied to the patriarchs and prophets in the Bible. It was during times of fasting that many of the great deliverances recorded in Scripture happened. It was during times of fasting God advanced people into greatness. It was during times of fasting God ushered in new eras. The Holy Spirit first came to the Jewish nation at Jerusalem to a group of people who had been fasting. The Holy Spirit also first revealed Himself among the gentiles to a group of people who had been fasting. Fasting defined great people such as Moses, Elijah, Daniel, and even Jesus himself. It is fasting that will also bring the greatest definition to our lives.

There is no scriptural mandate on the amount of time and effort that we spend doing these things. His desire is for us to seek Him with everything. However, God didn't make us robots; He gave us choices. The victory we experience in the day-to-day struggle is directly affected by our consistency in these things. If we are serious about overcoming our old sinful nature, we will be serious in our commitment to God.

Becoming More Like Him

According to Scripture, Jesus is the incarnate Word. The Gospel of John declares that "the Word was made flesh and dwelt among us" (1:14). Revelation 19 teaches us that the "Word of God" is another name for Jesus. Also, 1 John 1 calls Jesus the "Word of Life." In other words, the life of Jesus in every way lives out the Word of God. We are also intended to be infused with the Word of God. Paul explained to the Corinthian church that the church is the "Epistle of Christ, not written on tablets of stone, but on fleshly tablets of the heart" (2 Corinthians 3:3). In other words, we should also be incarnations of the Word of God. Maybe you have heard someone say, "We are the only Bible some will ever read." Just as Jesus fully represented the Father on this earth, we should fully represent Jesus. We should be the living, breathing, and moving image of Christ. Second Corinthians 4:6 says. "For God, who commanded the light to shine out of darkness, hath shined in our hearts, to give the light of the knowledge of the glory of God in the face of Jesus Christ."

This comparison of the creation story to our enlightenment explains how God uses the transformation process to shine the glory of God to us and through us. When God shines His glory into our hearts, He does it through the glorification of Jesus. This is the revelation process. When exposed to the glory of God, we shine with the light of the glory of God. Just like the moon has no light of its own, but reflects wonderfully the light of the sun; likewise, we have no glory of our own, but reflect the glory of God. We become the means for the initial experience with God for those who have never experienced Him. We point them to Christ, and then God begins to shine through them. Second Peter 1:19 says, "Ye do well that ye take heed, as unto a light that shineth in a dark place, until the day dawn, and the day star arise in your hearts."

When we cast off our old image and take on the image of the one who redeemed us, this is the transformation process. This change isn't superficial. It begins in the heart and moves outward. As we continue feeding on God's presence, the change becomes more obvious until we resemble the Lord in behavior and thought. Without the initiation of this process, we will perpetuate our old worldly image. Colossians 1:27 tells us that Christ being in us is the hope of glory. The reflection of God in our lives is the very thing that tears down the walls of the Enemy and begins to restore hope to the world.

After the transformation process takes root, God begins working through our lives to fulfill His own will. God can do anything. He doesn't need us, but He has chosen us to be the means by which He reveals Himself to the world. Ephesians 3:19-21 says, ". . . that ye might be filled with all the fulness of God. Now unto him that is able to do exceeding abundantly above all that we ask or think, according to the power that worketh in us, Unto him be glory in the church by Christ Jesus . . ."

This Scripture tells us two distinct things—the fullness of God is from God, and in us. We are His vessels. Paul allowed the power of God to work in him, yet he reminded us that we are just clay jars so we would remember to give God the glory. We know that being in Christ, and Christ being in us, is our spiritual vitality. However, all of this comes with one supreme condition. Matthew 16:24 instructs: "If any man will come after me, let him deny himself, and take up his cross, and follow me."

There must be a willingness to totally sell out to Christ. Satan wants us to equate serving Christ with losing out on life. On the contrary, our old nature keeps us from real life. Gaining Christ is gaining everything that pertains to life and true living. Our relationship with Christ is the only important item in the scope of eternity. If we crucify the old man within, we win Christ, and the glory of God comes alive in us. Nothing else in life is greater. When we are transformed into the image of the glory of God, life gains vibrancy and meaning. Spiritual emptiness fades, and we become strong and satisfied. Satan loses ground in our lives where he once held strongholds. The past struggles become distant memories. Life, peace, and happiness take hold. In short, Satan loses, and we win. First John 5:18 reads: "he that is begotten of God keepeth himself, and that wicked one toucheth him not."

The focus of this book has been overcoming the attacks of Satan. An attack of Satan is anything designed to separate us from God or any of His promises. However, the previous verse explains to us that there is a place in Christ that reaches beyond the hands of Satan. Still, he uses every possible thing to bring devastation into our lives, but if God be for us, nothing and no one can be against us." As we take advantage of living in Christ, God makes us the people He intends us to be. By being transformed into the image of the glory of God, we realize what it means to be more than conquerors. Total victory is the outcome of total surrender. At the moment of total surrender, we will finally be able to allow God to have His perfect will in us. If we are transformed by the power and glory of Jesus Christ, then Satan has no way to stop us from rising to that wonderful place found in Christ. What will Satan do if, when he comes knocking, Jesus answers the door? Place Jesus at the door of your heart. The power of God in you will be the very thing that God uses to destroy Satan's lullaby.

Prayer:
"Lord change us. Make us the people You would have us to be. Do whatever it takes. Not our will, but Yours be done."

TRANSFORMATION

Questions for Thought:

1. Is there a special calling on everyone's life?

2. God must carry us down a road that leads to total
   _____.

3. Why can experiencing God's glory sometimes make
   us feel uncomfortable?

4. Name four biblical characters from this chapter
   whose life was defined or transformed by fasting.

5. When God shines His glory into our hearts, He does
   it through the glorification of _____.

6. In what part of our being does the transformation
   process begin?

7. Total victory is the outcome of total
   _____.

Looking Back:
- Understand the process by which a believer is
  transformed into the person God desires him or her
  to be.
- Know that a total transformation will lead to being
  molded after the character of God himself.
- Be aware of the spiritual benefits of going through
  the transformation process.

  He that dwelleth in the secret place of the most High
  shall abide under the shadow of the Almighty. I will
  say of the Lord, He is my refuge and my fortress:

my God; in him will I trust. Surely he shall deliver thee from the snare of the fowler, and from the noisome pestilence. He shall cover thee with his feathers, and under his wings shalt thou trust: his truth shall be thy shield and buckler. Thou shalt not be afraid for the terror by night; nor for the arrow that flieth by day; Nor for the pestilence that walketh in darkness; nor for the destruction that wasteth at noonday. A thousand shall fall at thy side, and ten thousand at thy right hand; but it shall not come nigh thee. Only with thine eyes shalt thou behold and see the reward of the wicked. Because thou hast made the Lord, which is my refuge, even the most High, thy habitation; There shall no evil befall thee, neither shall any plague come nigh thy dwelling. For he shall give his angels charge over thee, to keep thee in all thy ways. They shall bear thee up in their hands, lest thou dash thy foot against a stone. Thou shalt tread upon the lion and adder: the young lion and dragon shalt thou trample under feet. Because he hath set his love upon me, therefore will I deliver him: I will set him on high, because he hath known my name. He shall call upon me, and I will answer him: I will be with him in trouble; I will deliver him, and honour him. With long life will I satisfy him, and shew him my salvation (Psalm 91).

www.ingramcontent.com/pod-product-compliance
Lightning Source LLC
Chambersburg PA
CBHW061958040426
42447CB00010B/1813